PRACTICAL WISDOMS @ WORK

PRACTICAL WISDOMS @Work™

Navigating the present
with a plan for the future

**KRISTINA M. OLSON
LYNN M. WHITBECK
RACHEL H. WHITBECK**

PO Box 504
Lopez Island, WA 98261

ACKNOWLEDGEMENTS

Practical Wisdoms @ Work started as a desire to build a bridge—a bridge to enable two BFFs to work together again, and a bridge to give back to the young women in the workforce. Along our paths of 30-plus-year careers, there are so many experiences, mistakes, triumphs, uncomfortable situations, aha-s, and in-group knowledge you only acquire during the journey. *Practical Wisdoms @ Work* is our venue to share our "been there, done that" moments with tips, ideas, mindful awareness, and constructive alternatives to conquer the challenges young women will likely face at work.

Getting it down on paper and organized into a digital file would have been impossible without Amanda and Rachel Whitbeck. Amanda got us started with free-form interviews. This enabled us to organize our thoughts into a structure and compartmentalized process. Once we had our map, Amanda put our thoughts, insights, and experiences into a more cohesive mold. Our transition from Amanda to Rachel was a perfect novella of common work experience. Work is always a series of changes, moving parts, and serendipity. Rachel was that serendipitous element. Rachel brought disruptive innovation, challenging and pushing us for relevant examples and insights to refine *Practical Wisdoms @ Work*. Rachel was the catalyst that brought everything together. She expertly distilled our message into coherence.

Our amazing publicist, Steve Fisher, provided us with our initial, decisive feedback. He supported us in setting the tone and pace for *Practical Wisdoms @ Work*. After we had our draft completed, Steve was our sounding board, sharing our enthusiasm and objectives. We were also tremendously fortunate to have our good friend and peer Liz Jones review the content. Liz was invaluable, providing us with insightful and constructive input.

Along with Amanda and Steve, Alison Rollins, Alexis Pellegrino, and Bruce and Francesca Bennett helped us with the final review prior to publication. Everyone shared in our respect for our message and our audience. We could not have accomplished this without you.

TINA

Writing *Practical Wisdoms @ Work* has been a fulfilling journey. Traveling back in time to recapture lessons learned—both positive and challenging—has strengthened my spirit and confidence in a life open to new experiences and adventures.

I am appreciative of the broad opportunities and moral foundation provided by the love and support of my family. They are always top of mind in my actions and deeds.

I would be remiss to not mention those colleagues and clients from whom I have learned—I cherish our continued relationships. I am also forever grateful to those with whom I share a heart and passion for helping those in need.

Thank you to both Lynn and Rachel; it has been a privilege working with them on this project.

LYNN

Writing *Practical Wisdoms @ Work* has been such an incredible experience, as was working with an amazing team who shared a vision of sharing knowledge with young women. It has been a true labor of love. The opportunity to work with Tina again has been rewarding in so many ways. I would not have thought it possible, but my admiration and respect for her evolved and strengthened during this journey.

The wonderful women in my life have been such a vital influence, it's hard to ever adequately express. My mother, Shirley, is always there for me, and a BFF in the truest sense. My aunties JoAnn, Linda, and Karen have all been so important in my life. These incredible, brilliant, loving women have encouraged me and supported me through the years with wisdom and grace.

On a personal note, this book reflects my hopes and love for the three most important young women in my life, daughter Francesca and nieces Amanda and Rachel. My daughter has been, and continues to be, my rock and closest confidant. With their help and support we will truly shatter the glass ceiling. Break it down to the sand it came from! You go, girls!

Finally, to my father Jerry Whitbeck and husband Bruce Bennett: You made this possible. Unfortunately, both passed before publication. My father was my first mentor—in life and at work. He continued in that role throughout my life, sharing his wisdom and offering a guiding hand. My husband, Bruce, has been my partner in the truest sense. My sounding board, shoulder to cry on, and number one cheerleader. This book would not have been possible without his loving support and overwhelming belief in me.

RACHEL

Thank you to Amanda, who left me with a clear roadmap and a solid foundation to move forward with the book. As my big sister, Amanda has always led by example, forging a path and showing me how to build my own future. As with this book, Amanda offers me guidance whenever I ask for it (and sometimes when I don't) and is generous with her support.

Amanda and I were both following the example of our mother, Suzanne Whitbeck. She taught us how to be likeable, how to work hard, how to be fashionable, how to lead, and how to find the humor in dark situations. My mom also provided me with one of the stories in this book, demonstrating how being helpful is rewarded in the workplace. She told Amanda and me that we could be anything, and I believe the same of her.

A myriad of women—family, friends, teachers, and colleagues—have demonstrated how to live my life successfully. My three aunts, two grandmothers, many cousins (first, second, third; once, twice removed); my friends from all walks of life; my co-workers and supervisors have all imparted their wisdom, directly and indirectly. I am grateful for it.

Practical Wisdoms @ Work. Copyright © by Kristina M. Olson, Lynn M. Whitbeck, & Rachel H. Whitbeck. Manufactured in the United States of America. All rights reserved. No part of this book may be reproduced or transmitted in any form or by any means, electronic or mechanical, including photocopying, recording, or by an information storage and retrieval system -- except by a reviewer, who may quote brief passages in a review to be printed in a magazine, newspaper, or on the Web -- without permission in writing from the publisher. Published by Petite2Queen, PO Box 504, Lopez Island, WA 98261. First Edition.

Although the authors and publisher have made every effort to ensure the accuracy and completeness of information contained in this book, we assume no responsibility for errors, inaccuracies, omissions, or any inconsistency herein. Any slights of people, places, or organizations are unintentional. First printing 2017.

For more resources and practical wisdoms, visit Petite2Queen.com.

To receive a free weekly email newsletter delivering tips, updates, and practical wisdoms, register directly at http://Petite2Queen.com/subscribe.

ISBN 978-0-9995172-2-2
Library of Congress Control Number: 2017957352

Cover design by: SB
Photograph by: Irina Logra
Edited by: Amanda Whitbeck, Alison Rollins, Elizabeth Jones, Steve Fisher, and Alexis Pellegrino.
Production coordinated by: Heather McIntyre, Cover&Layout

ATTENTION CORPORATIONS, UNIVERSITIES, COLLEGES, AND PROFESSIONAL ORGANIZATIONS: Quantity discounts are available on bulk purchases of this book for educational, gift purchases, or as premiums for increasing magazine subscriptions or renewals. Special books or book excerpts can also be created to fit specific needs. For information, please contact Petite2Queen, PO Box 504, Lopez Island, WA 98261.

PRACTICAL WISDOMS @ WORK

CONTENTS

Introduction	1
Chapter 1	7
Embarking on Your Journey	
Chapter 2	15
Building & Embracing Success	
Chapter 3	25
Making Yourself Indispensable	
Chapter 4	37
Work-Life Balance & Boundaries	
Chapter 5	49
Time Management	
Chapter 6	61
Stress Management	
Chapter 7	71
Networking	
Chapter 8	81
Friend vs. Business Relationship	
Chapter 9	91
Dealing with Difficult People	
Chapter 10	99
Bullying & Harassment at Work	
Chapter 11	109
Mentors & Support Structures	
Chapter 12	117
Breaking Double Standards	
Chapter 13	127
Leadership Styles	
Chapter 14	137
Find Fulfillment & Feed Your Soul	
Conclusion	143
About the Authors	147
References	149

INTRODUCTION

Women have been entering the workforce in droves for decades, and they are here to stay. While women have *always* worked, they began to fully participate in the labor market in the 20th century. Today, women have permeated nearly every career and most every position in existence. Making this progress has taken a lot of hard work by generations of women.

The workforce is more educated today than it was just a few decades ago. While all demographics are attaining more education than previous generations, it's women who have made the largest strides. In 1970, 20% of men and 12% of women ages 25 to 32 had 4-year degrees.[1] Contrast this with 2013, when those numbers increased to 31% of men and 38% of women in the same age group having at least a four-year college degree.[2] Also in 2013, 45% of women and 38% of men ages 18 to 24 were enrolled in college.

This education, along with other factors, have cleared the way for millions of women to work. In 2016, the Pew Research Center announced that the number of millennials in the workforce surpassed the number of workers among baby boomers or Generation X. Young people currently number 75.4 million workers.[3] In 2013, 54% of the young professional force was made up of women.[4] If women still made up 54% of the millennial workforce in 2016, they would have numbered over 40.7 million workers—that's impressive!

And as women increase their ranks within the workplace, progress is being made regarding pay, as well. Between 1980 and 2012, women have increased their pay parity with men from making 65% of what men make for the same work to 84%; millennial women make 93% of what their male

---

[1] http://www.pewsocialtrends.org/2013/12/11/10-findings-about-women-in-the-workplace/
[2] http://www.pewsocialtrends.org/2013/12/11/on-pay-gap-millennial-women-near-parity-for-now/
[3] http://www.pewresearch.org/fact-tank/2016/04/25/millennials-overtake-baby-boomers/
[4] http://dpeaflcio.org/programs-publications/issue-fact-sheets/the-young-professional-workforce/

counterparts earn![5] Still, 84% or 93%, it's not enough. In 2013, 67% of American workers believed that there was more work to be done for gender equality at work. This included 77% of female baby boomers and 75% of millennial women. Even the majority in of men in these cohorts agree![6]

As we do the work for greater gender parity, the CEOs and founders of Petite2Queen, Lynn and Tina, as well as Director of Operations and Communications Rachel, see no reason for young women to reinvent the wheel over and over as they enter the workforce. Instead, we would like to see women share the wisdom and skills they've gained during their careers with the young women who may need it today.

WHY WE WROTE THIS BOOK

While many things have changed over the decades, a lot of things have stayed the same. Between the two of them, Lynn and Tina have 75 years of experience, and they decided that they could give young women a hand up in their careers. After all, Sir Isaac Newton got to "stand on the shoulders of giants" to make his mathematical and scientific discoveries; you should be able to stand on someone's shoulders, too, as you make your mark in the world.

Over the course of their careers, Tina and Lynn have made mistakes and breakthroughs. The way we see it, there is no need for you to repeat their mistakes *or* their breakthroughs. We want you to start with the lessons Lynn and Tina have learned so that you can go forward and make your *own* mistakes and breakthroughs. That way you'll have your own practical wisdoms to pass on. By offering each other advice and experience, women will keep moving forward on their journey toward excellence.

We wrote this book so that you will have somewhere to look for advice when you face challenges and opportunities in your career. Tina and Lynn have been through many difficult situations—similar to yours and not—and have gained valuable wisdom and skills to help with the next crossroads in their careers. We hope that this wisdom and these skills will be of use throughout your journey, as well.

---

[5] http://www.pewsocialtrends.org/2013/12/11/on-pay-gap-millennial-women-near-parity-for-now/; this article does not break down the differences among the different races and ethnicities of women in their pay rate.
[6] Ibid.

HOW TO USE THIS BOOK

Practical Wisdoms @ Work is a resource for women who are entering the workforce and building their careers. The advice and wisdoms contained in this volume are garnered from the experiences of Lynn, Tina, Rachel, and our friends and family. Our words are not gospel and should not be taken as such. This book is filled with what we learned through our own trials and tribulations—lessons that we've found useful in our careers. So, use our experience as guidance as you find what works for you. With *Practical Wisdoms @ Work*, you don't need to start at square one as you forge your own path and work out your own solutions. Try out our advice, and see what fits.

This book starts at the beginning with *Chapter 1: Embarking on Your Journey* guides you through finding your path and dealing with the detours. We know that many careers have false starts, unexpected turns, and roadblocks; we're here to help you figure out what to do in each case.

Chapter 2: Building & Embracing Success covers the broad skills you will need as a foundation to a successful career, such as pushing yourself, being attentive, and continuing to learn. Things start to get more specific in *Chapter 3: Making Yourself Indispensable*, which discusses how to gain positive attention in the workplace by volunteering for new projects, exuding confidence, being helpful, and more. All of this will make you more competitive for promotions and new opportunities.

With *Chapter 4: Work-Life Balance & Boundaries*, we recognize that careers sometimes have a tendency to try to take over one's life. Within these pages, we discuss how you can distance yourself from work when you clock out, despite all of our gadgets keeping us connected to our bosses and colleagues. Related to this, *Chapter 5: Time Management* gives you tips and tricks to keep all your tasks—professional and personal— on track. We talk about how to avoid procrastination, but also what to do if things get away from you. This chapter also discusses how to best work at home, where distractions can abound. *Chapter 6: Stress Management* follows up with how to manage, express, and minimize your stress, and what to do when your stress gets the better of you.

We at Petite2Queen believe that our relationships are the foundation of all things in life, including our careers. *Chapter 7: Networking* covers that all-important skill, showing you why networks are important, how to find the courage to start your network, and how to maintain those relationships. In maintaining those relationships, the nature of the relationships might get fuzzy; *Chapter 8: Friend vs. Business Relationship* discusses the possible ways you might want to keep these two groups separate, and the ways you might want to mix them.

Not all business relationships are sunshine and roses, of course. *Chapter 9: Dealing with Difficult People* gives you the tools to deal with the unmotivated, the uncommunicative, and the downright nasty people you may encounter throughout your career. For situations that go beyond simple unpleasant behavior, though, we have *Chapter 10: Bullying & Harassment at Work*. How to survive a bully, deal with sexual harassment, and prevent yourself from engaging in bullying behavior are the topics here.

Chapter 11: Mentors & Support Structures teaches you how to find the people who will help you grow and succeed in your career, either by showing you the ropes or giving you reprieve from the daily grind. We also draw from our own experience on how to become a mentor yourself and provide a helping hand to the ones who will come after you.

Chapter 12: Breaking Double Standards helps you to fight back against sexism and bias in the workplace by making yourself heard, calling out unfair practices, and changing the culture of the office, if you must. Breaking through barriers includes becoming a leader, and our *Chapter 13: Leadership Styles* helps you navigate this path. It starts with a discussion of the different leadership styles you are likely to encounter in your career, including when certain methods work and don't work. This way, you can identify not only the types of leaders you most want to work with, but the ones you want to emulate as a leader.

Practical Wisdoms @ Work closes with *Chapter 14: Find Fulfillment & Feed Your Soul*. While careers are a major part of many people's dreams, it's important to avoid burnout. These last pages reflect on how you can make your job gratifying— even when it's not the one you wanted—and how to find satisfaction outside of your work. After all, you need to take care of your whole self, not just the career woman in you.

GOING FORWARD

Women's presence in the workplace is growing, and it's clear that that's not going to change. The women of decades past have paved the way for this rising generation, and millennials will continue to push the progress further. As we move forward, the best strategy is for women who have been there and done that to help the ones who are currently facing the obstacles of new employment.

Practical Wisdoms @ Work is here to help with that process as we offer advice and stories from Lynn and Tina, with some insights from Rachel, about how to be successful in a career. Find in these pages the inspiration and guidance to keeping climbing toward your dreams. You go!

CHAPTER 1
EMBARKING ON YOUR JOURNEY

YOU ARE IN the early stages of your career path. Maybe you're just starting college, in your first job, or have been in your career for years, but if you are considered a millennial, you are still in the Early Career section of your Wikipedia page. Embarking on this journey can seem daunting, but with the right tools and attitudes, you can build your life and work into something great. So, how do you get started? What difficulties might you face? How can you stay true to yourself? We're here to help you answer those questions.

FINDING YOUR PATH

The first step in your journey to success is to identify your destination. The second step is planning how you'll get there. They sound so easy when you see them written out like this, but these steps can be some of your most difficult. The seemingly simple task of knowing what you want can be overwhelming for some people, and you will need to find a way to zero in on your passions and desires.

Some people seem like they're just born knowing what they want to do. Like the aspiring police officer Judy Hopps in *Zootopia*, they declare their dream career in elementary school, and they stick to it until they finally achieve their goals. Those are the minority of people. Most of us have to look a little harder to find a field that fulfills us; some of us find it in high school, some in college, some have to work a few jobs before we find it, and some don't have our "aha!" moment until well into our career. Everyone's road to self-discovery is different.

The easiest way to find out your ideal career is to try new things. Think you might be interested in computer programming? Try learning some code. Does acting sound like the perfect job? Perform at your community theater. You can take classes, find volunteer work, or get jobs in almost anything these days. Give it a shot, and see if it's something you would want to do for a living.

> ### FROM PRE-MED TO HISTORY
> In high school and the first year of college, I wanted to be a doctor; I wanted to be the best, and when someone asked what I was going to do when I grew up, "doctor" sounded impressive to me. During college, I realized that medicine was not my passion—at all. I knew I had to change course, and I discovered how much history fascinated me. I became a history major.
>
> While I have never worked a day in my life in a job in any way related to history, what I learned in all those history courses directly translated into strong business skills that I use to this day: There are rarely (if ever) simple, one-dimensional answers, and working through a difficult situation can bring about positive change and move us forward. – **Lynn**

Once you've figured out what you want to do, you need to plan how you're going to do it. If you want to be a doctor, you should plan on going to medical school. Other careers have more choices in how you reach your goals. To be a novelist, you might choose to get a degree or take classes in creative writing. You could start by submitting short stories to literary magazines, or you might go straight to shopping your novel around to different publishing houses—or go ahead and publish it yourself!

Sometimes the myriad of different paths you can follow to reach your goal can be overwhelming. Focus on what you can realistically do based on your personal needs and resources, as well as which direction seems the most exciting or appealing. There is no "right" avenue to follow, only the best one *for you*. Just as with determining your best field in the first place, you might explore different methods of achieving your goals until you find the path that makes the most sense to you.

GIVE IT A SHOT
Now that you have a goal and a plan of action, the next might be obvious: try it. You have to put in the work to get results, so start now. Figure out exactly what steps you'll take, and then

prepare to take them. Do your research and get ahead of the ball, or you'll find yourself having to retread your path again and again until you get it right.

While some lucky few get success handed to them, most of us have to work hard for what we get, and, depending on the distance we're traveling, some of us have to work harder than others. Ask for help when you need it—from teachers, mentors, friends, family, and professional communities—but also learn how to do your own research and find your own answers.

These days, the journey to your career success isn't likely to be easy. Unpaid internships and "entry-level" jobs that require years of experience are the norm in many fields.[1,2] College is expensive, often prohibitively so, and debt follows so many of those who extend their education after high school.[3,4] Wages have remained stagnant while living costs have risen, leaving workers with less and less ability to save.[5]

Why are we telling you this? This book contains a lot of optimism because we believe that anyone can achieve their goals, but we also want to be realistic about the landscape out there. There may be more obstacles to overcome or work around to reach your dreams. With the right tools and the right attitude, you can make it.

So try. Give it 100% because you deserve to live a fulfilled life. Understand that there will be challenges, and work those into your plans to build your best career. Doing this will develop your skills in problem solving and resourcefulness, and you will become a stronger candidate within your field because of it. With a clear but flexible plan in mind, work hard and persevere until you reach your goals.

NAVIGATING ROAD BLOCKS

Of course, "work hard and plan well" aren't enough to avoid obstacles or keep you from making mistakes. Like all of us,

---

1 http://www.theatlantic.com/business/archive/2012/05/work-is-work-why-free-internships-are-immoral/257130/
2 http://www.wsj.com/articles/want-an-entry-level-job-youll-need-lots-of-experience-1407267498
3 http://www.usnews.com/education/best-colleges/paying-for-college/articles/2015/07/29/chart-see-20-years-of-tuition-growth-at-national-universities
4 http://www.huffingtonpost.com/kyle-mccarthy/10-fun-facts-about-student-loan-debt_b_4639044.html
5 http://www.pewresearch.org/fact-tank/2014/10/09/for-most-workers-real-wages-have-barely-budged-for-decades/

you will fail, and you may fail repeatedly. You will also face roadblocks during your journey that seem insurmountable. In these cases, the urge might be to give up, shut down, and go to bed. Do give yourself a break and take that nap, but always get back up and keep going.

Let's begin with the roadblocks. Sometimes, even when you do everything right, there will be a surprise that will throw you off track and on a path you didn't imagine. Sometimes you just get stuck behind this immovable obstacle and feel like you can't go through it, over it, or around it. What do you do?

A SERIES OF UNFORTUNATE EVENTS

While my plans have shifted over time, they've always been focused on academia. Any real path to my goal involved getting good grades in college. During my first two years as an undergrad, I worked hard and did very well. I was proud of myself.

Between my sophomore and junior years, a series of tragedies struck. I was transferring universities, my dad suddenly died, the house I grew up in was foreclosed and my mom and I were forced out. To top it all off, our cat Pumpkin died. I don't know how we dealt with all of it.

I had already been managing anxiety before all this, but these events put me in a deep depression. I missed classes and fell behind on assignments. My GPA dropped an entire point in just one semester. Despite all this, I knew that I still wanted to follow my dreams to become a professor.

My course forward began by talking with my academic advisor and setting up a new plan. I withdrew from two classes the second semester of my junior year, got extensions in two more, and only completed one class on time. I reevaluated the amount of work I could handle, and, with my advisor, decided that I should take a smaller course load at a time. I had to take two summer semesters to graduate on my original schedule. But I did it, and I was able to bring my GPA back up to something I could be proud of. **– Rachel**

Sometimes you're hit with things you can't control, like in the story above. Remember that while you can't always control the circumstances, you always have power over yourself and how you respond to it. Take a moment to evaluate your needs and capabilities, as well as your support systems and resources, and decide how to move forward. Maybe you'll keep on your same path, but at a slower pace, or perhaps you'll choose a new path altogether that will be a better fit.

THE WRONG CHORD
I've always had an affinity for playing the piano, and I have had a piano since early childhood. It was my grandparents who encouraged me to pursue lessons as it was clearly something that I enjoyed, and my grandparents supported my interests. I received many awards for my accomplishments.

In college, I decided to minor in music. Unfortunately, I was assigned to a professor that did not train in the manner I was used to. We had a complete disconnect. She felt that I lacked talent, and rather than argue, I admitted defeat and resigned from the program (regardless of my established success). In true dramatic fashion, I threw out my music and informed my grandparents that I would not play the piano again.

After a period of about five years, I began playing again—much to my enjoyment and that of my grandparents! Looking back, that professor had a huge impact on me and my future. It says more about the person I was then—unassertive and impressionable—that would enable someone to have a significant impact on me. I'm sure had another professor been an option, my path would have looked completely different. **– Tina**

Sometimes a failed attempt will be your own fault. Perhaps you didn't prepare enough or didn't fully understand the requirements or didn't ask the right questions. Whatever the reason, your proposal gets rejected, your project gets ruined, or you experience any number of possible failures.

In these cases, the first step you should take is owning up to your mistake. By admitting your error, you will show yourself to be honest—a trait peers and managers appreciate. Apologize, *mean* it, and *rectify the situation*. Apologies mean nothing if you simply go on to repeat your misbehavior again and again in the future. Identify what you could have done better, learn from your mistakes, and demonstrate your new knowledge at the next opportunity. Even if it's not with the same company, you can at least show yourself that you have learned your lesson. This in itself can be satisfying.

Regardless of where the roadblocks come from, remember that these are all just steps on your journey to your dream career. Every time you're thrown off track, look at it as a learning moment. Gain new wisdom and continue to move forward. You're one step closer to success!

DETOURS AND OPPORTUNITIES

Throughout your career and life, new opportunities will appear in unexpected places. Some you will seek out, others will drop in your lap, and still others will have always been present, awaiting your notice. Be open to these new possibilities, and recognize that they will come in different forms. Finding a new opportunity can be as simple as having a conversation with a friend or a colleague who mentions a new project they're working on. If you find it interesting, ask more about it, and see how you can get involved.

A good way to discover new opportunities is to follow your interests. If you hear about something that fascinates you, ask about it. Curiosity is what creates opportunities—opportunities for improvement and enrichment, in work and in life.

But what if the opportunity doesn't fit within the plan in our head? Very few of us follow our original plan from start to finish; careers don't take a linear track. Instead, you will find your path to be more like a hydrangea—each petal is a different idea, passion, person, and opportunity, but they all come together to create the whole. It's important to stay open to new possibilities and to think outside of the box. Only by shaking up your paradigm will you see new paths and choices. Enjoy the journey, and take the side roads and detours that make sense. The new experiences awaiting you may be just what you have been seeking.

BEING YOUR AUTHENTIC SELF

Being honest is the best way to get where you want to go. You have to begin by being honest with yourself about what you want, and then you have to be true to yourself throughout the journey. Your morals and values are things to hold onto while you're on your path to success because they will make you stand out, and your authenticity will color everything you do.

Besides feeling more fulfilled as a person, being honest and authentic will make you more successful. The most obvious way is that people are more willing to trust honest people, and people like to work with people they can trust. As we mentioned in the last section, one way to express your honesty is by owning up to your mistakes, as well as giving credit where it's due. Peers and supervisors appreciate that sort of straightforwardness, and they will be more likely to believe you when you take credit for a job well done.

Authenticity can help you in other, less direct ways, too. As we will discuss in more detail in *Chapter 7*, networking is an important part of career-building. As you connect with clients, customers, and peers in your field, being your unguarded self will help you create meaningful relationships. Being authentic allows you to have deeper conversations with people, and it allows your conversational partner to be authentic, as well. Without those barriers up, peers will be far more comfortable talking with you and connecting with you.

Of course, there are some limits to your honesty. The goal is to be empathetic and authentic, but there is no need to over-share. As always, avoid politics and religion when speaking with professional connections and colleagues. It is good to be honest about when you're having a bad day or are in a bad humor—you don't always need to be chipper—but you should always aim to be polite.

RECAP

You've started working on the first two steps of your career journey: choosing a destination and a path. We've discussed obstacles and authenticity. When you're blazing your trail, ask yourself the following questions:

1. Do you have a dream career? What things would you like to try, and how can you try them? What will you need to do to reach your dreams?
2. Which obstacles will you have to face on your journey? How will you persevere?
3. When life throws you off track, what steps can you take to manage your new path? How can you learn from your mistakes?

4. What are your values and morals, and how can you stay true to them? How can you let down your barriers when talking to peers?

PLAYLIST

For inspiration as you begin your journey, listen to our playlist at: http://p2q.link/chapter1

CHAPTER 2
BUILDING & EMBRACING SUCCESS

ONCE YOU'VE FOUND your passions and entered the workforce, it's time to start paying attention to the things that make you who you are. What makes you unique? What skills and knowledge do you bring with you? On the flip side, what skills and knowledge are you lacking? It's always important to take in your surroundings and see how you fit in and where you stand out. Let's look at the ways you can make sure you're always presenting the best version of yourself.

AIM FOR EXCELLENCE

An important lesson to learn is that you should always try your best. Don't be satisfied with being mediocre. If you have the choice to accept where you are or keep pushing forward, don't choose complacency. Aim to be your best self.

The people you work with, and certainly your supervisors and managers, can spot talent... and they can identify slackers—those who do as little as possible and don't pull their weight. You don't want to be seen as such. Go above and beyond, and your peers will take notice. If you want to get ahead, you have to prove that you deserve it and have the determination to work for it.

Ambition leads to greatness. Success has no time for those who are not driven to keep improving, learning, and striving to be their best. You can always improve somewhere, and you should aim to be your best. If you're not doing your best, you won't be a leader in your company or industry. It's also important to keep in mind that this is an ongoing process. You can always learn more about a subject and think bigger—don't stop just because you think you've reached the top. Stay curious and current: follow trends, technology, and new ideas.

While you are on your path to greatness, be careful not to overwork yourself or drive yourself to exhaustion. Pace yourself. Be able to accept that no one can be perfect. You can only do *your* best. Give yourself balance; make time for friends and family, hobbies, exercise, and enough sleep. Don't settle, but don't hold yourself to unrealistic expectations. Be happy and confident in yourself, know that you are enough, and just make sure you are happy with your efforts and commitments, and remember to celebrate your small successes along the way.

BUILD RELATIONSHIPS

You know what they say: There's no "I" in "team." Well, there's no "I" in "success," either. If you're going to be successful in work and life, you'll need to accept that you can't do it alone. You will need to build quality relationships with those higher up the corporate ladder, lower on said ladder, and those on an entirely different ladder. You'll have to get along with people and be genuine because there's another adage you've probably heard countless times: It's not what you know, it's who you know. And that door goes both ways.

When you're at work, take the time to get to know your co-workers. Talk to them, get to know their working styles and personal interests, and try to make genuine connections. Learn about the things they are passionate about and what they know. It is great to talk with someone that has been there when you are venturing down new avenues. Even if you don't become close friends, having positive relationships is important in finding success.

These connections will grow, develop, and, if nurtured, can play a role in your future success. They can attest to your skills, efficiency, and integrity, and the better impression people have of you, the more they will want to work with you. Interact through professional social channels, such as LinkedIn, to further strengthen your network. The people you know may advance in their careers or move to another company, and if they have a good relationship with you, there is a better chance that they will consider you for new and more challenging opportunities with them. When you're interested in a new job opportunity, your reputation will precede you. What kind of reputation do you want to build?

When you're talking with your co-workers and other professionals, always remember to be genuine. Don't talk with the goal of "kissing up" or "brown-nosing"—not only can people see right through that calculated, fake act, you also won't be truly connecting with the person. No one wants to work with someone who doesn't seem authentic; they are less trustworthy, and it's impossible to really know them. Be honest and open.

We shouldn't even have to say this, but be kind to everyone, not just people you think are important. No matter who a person is or what position they hold within a company, be kind. It's been said that you can glean a person's true character by how she treats waiters or other service workers. Always be polite, patient, kind, respectful, and compassionate.

Getting to know your co-workers while on the job is a great start, but don't stop there! Participate in company events when your work is finished. Attend business networking events. Strive to meet new people and make valuable connections. Networking is an important key to success, and even if you're shy or awkward, it's a valuable step in building your potential for success. You want people to know you.

THE FINE ART OF SMALL TALK

Once upon a time, one of the things I loathed was attending business events where I either knew no one or only a few people. This especially included going to the networking events at conferences. Then one day, one hour transformed my attitude, my approach, and my enjoyment of these occasions. It was the equivalent of a lightning strike.

It was the kick off session at a conference presented by Debra Fine, author of The Fine Art of Small Talk. She told us about her own experience of hating these events and "hiding" in a corner or behind a colleague. She talked about how she realized she needed to change and how she did it.

As she went through her presentation, I saw myself and realized how much I wanted to change and stop allowing my fears to control my behavior. For the rest of the event I practiced everything she had presented. And my conference experience was amazing!

> *Ever since that kick-off session with Debra Fine, I eagerly anticipate every business event and conference. It was life changing. I passionately recommend* The Fine Art of Small Talk *for anyone who wants to stop being a wallflower and join in. Thank you, Debra Fine.* – **Lynn**

When you're socializing with people, try to have interesting things to talk about or ask about. Learn the art of small talk. The first step is to remember people's names; when you meet a new person and learn their name, repeat it back to them. One trick to better conversation is to ask the other person questions. Instead of dominating the conversation, make sure to let the other person talk. Ask them what they do, what they enjoy, who they know. Be a good listener. You'll be amazed at how quickly you can find a connection and common ground.

As you spend more time together, learn things about them—spouses' names, children, hobbies, etc. It is a good idea to write down this information in their contact profile to help you remember. When you talk to them in the future, be ready to ask about their life or to share some interesting information that they would be happy to know. They'll feel good that you remembered them and were thinking of them.

Remember, strong working relationships are built on trust, respect, and mindfulness. Recognizing and welcoming diversity of all types in your team validates each colleague's identity, experience, and ideas. This, in turn, encourages open communication among your co-workers—collaboration and conflict resolution become much easier tasks! Effective communication requires you to be an active listener so that you can understand your peers' needs, allowing you to deliver on time.

Relationships are vital to your success. People you know can ultimately lead you to new opportunities and more relationships, but remember to give more than you take. You can also help the people you know! Remember your co-workers and contacts, and maybe one day you'll be the one looking for a new business partner. Relationships go both ways, and when good fortune comes your way, you can pay it forward.

BE ATTENTIVE

This is a skill that can't be overstated. Your success relies largely on how attentive you are. Take responsibility for your words and actions. People that are responsible, stick to deadlines, and are responsive to communications are more likely to advance their careers. Be someone that others can count on and trust.

The first thing you should commit to is responding quickly. Anytime you get an email, voicemail, or other social media message, respond to it as soon as you are able. Not only is it polite, it also shows that you are interested and care about your work and team members. It's good practice to respond to people within one business day.

> **REPLY TO EVERY MESSAGE**
> *Early in my career, I would read about women in business whom I felt I would want to emulate. What could I do to better myself? One stand out was the story of a woman that ran a large movie studio, which, in that era, was highly unusual. What stood out to me in this article is that she felt that every message she received was important. It didn't matter who it was from, she felt that anyone who had tried to get in touch with her or tried to share information with her deserved the acknowledgement that they had done so. She would take the time before the end of every day to reply to each one personally.*
>
> *The story had a profound effect on me because her actions were so respectful. Here's a woman running a huge studio, with enormous responsibilities, but she made it a priority to respond to every inquiry. I have tried to follow her example. I think it's a tremendous work ethic, a terrific value, and demonstrates respect for others. She had an enormous impact on the way in which I do business.* **– Tina**

In addition to being a reliable professional, prompt responses can also help you attain opportunities. Sometimes a project or job comes up, and only those who answer within a certain amount of time will be considered. If you delay even for a few hours, you might lose a great opportunity to someone who acted more quickly.

Today, job applications depend on swiftness of response more than ever before. Many companies only consider those who apply within the first two or three days. Even the most qualified candidates may be overlooked simply because their application arrived later than the others. Remember, the early bird gets the worm or, in this case, the job opportunities.

Another point that can't be stressed enough is the importance of organization. This is good not only for your own peace of mind, but also for the time-sensitive needs of your colleagues. When you're working on a project, keep all documents and files related to it in one location. They should be easy to find and navigate. When your boss needs a file, you should be able to locate it and send it back quickly. If you lose track of where things are, that will slow down your ability to work and could cause issues with the quality of your work.

Good organization also means good time management. Be mindful of your appointments and schedule, and don't ever miss meetings or double book yourself because of a lapse in memory. Time is money, and if you can't keep track of your time and appointments, you may miss important opportunities or delay others' schedules. Manage your time for your own sanity and for the benefit of others. Always do what you say you're going to do when you say you're going to do it, and you will build up others' trust in you as a reliable employee. Effectively managing your time and responsibilities has the added bonus of helping you balance work and life.

If you make sure you're responsive and organized, you'll become a go-to person that others can depend on and turn to for important tasks. When your boss notices how quickly you respond to inquiries and how well you keep track of your work, she may think of you first when a new project comes up. Being the go-to person in your workplace will set you up for more opportunities... and more success.

KEEP LEARNING

You may already have that hard-earned degree, but just because you've left the classroom doesn't mean you're done learning. Quite the contrary; we need to make sure we never stop learning. Stay up-to-date about emerging trends, new ideas, and modern techniques, both within your realm of business and outside of it. You never know when your job will require a new perspective or additional duties, or when you can lead the way on a new path.

First, when you start with a new company, do your research about them and their industry. The more you know about your organization and its place in the grander scheme of things, the better prepared you will be to lead it to success. What is your company's history? What is their mission? How do they work, who do they work with, and how is that evolving? Do your best to fully understand where you work and what your role is.

Doctors learn all about medicine and procedures in college, but they can't stop learning there. If they did, doctors who graduated in the 1970s would have some very outdated medical practices! Doctors are required to continually update their knowledge as new medical discoveries are made. They continue to build on the knowledge they have and change what they thought they knew as better techniques, medications, and technologies develop.

Your career is much the same. You have to continue learning new things, sometimes adding to your arsenal of wisdom and sometimes rewriting what used to be common practice. Don't ever get stuck in the way things were. The world keeps moving forward, and so must you. Read as much as you can about anything related to your industry, as well as things outside of it. Perhaps learning a new skill will be valuable, in which case you can take a class or find some online tutorials. If you grow your knowledge, you'll be able to evolve in your career.

Be prepared for all kinds of twists and turns that may arise. If you're prepared and on top of all the latest trends and advances, you'll be positioned for success.

KEEP UP WITH EMERGING TRENDS

During my professional sales career, the industry I was in completely transformed. I recognized early on that I had to adapt, and adapt quickly. This could have been due to the number of times my family moved during my grade school years; I had to learn resiliency, flexibility, and how to keep moving forward.

As my industry evolved, I was constantly pushing to try new things, understand how technology was shaping our business, and how it could be leveraged. Rather than be satisfied with the status quo, I strived to be out front and engaged in the emerging trends. I worked hard and smart, and never settled. This drive to always do my very best was a tremendous asset and directly assisted my rapid rise within the company. **– Lynn**

ACCEPT SUCCESS

With all of your building blocks in place, you're well on your way to success. There is still one last mindset you'll need to adopt, though, so you can make it far: Allow yourself to be successful.

When you stumble upon a new opportunity, be ready to take it, even if you're not sure if you're ready for it. Even if you feel a little unprepared or nervous, go for it! Step outside your comfort zone, and try new things. You may uncover a new skill or passion that you want to pursue and master. It may lead to other exciting new opportunities that you'd never have encountered otherwise. At worst, you may find that it's not something you want to do, or something you need to practice in the future. We only grow when we get outside of our comfort zones and embrace new experiences.

However, don't take an opportunity just for the sake of saying you did it. It's also important to know yourself, what your values are, and where your skills lie. If your passion and expertise are in marketing, it might not make sense for you to pursue an opportunity in engineering. Choose your opportunities wisely, but fearlessly. If it is something you're interested in, by all means, go for it!

LESSONS FROM THE TANK

There is a television show called Shark Tank *in which entrepreneurs present their ideas to a team of extremely successful entrepreneurs. Contestants compete to get investments from one or more of the panel. It's a phenomenal class on business.*

What specifically stands out for me is the laser focus of the panel. Individually, they know what their talents are and the strength of their portfolio. If an idea is presented which is a fit for them, they might make an offer. More importantly, if a concept is not a good fit, they quickly acknowledge it and bow out.

Over the years, I have attempted to work with all people and most opportunities regardless of whether or not they fit into my organization's strengths or portfolio of services. By applying my newfound knowledge, I am learning to quickly identify a good fit and pursue it and just as quickly identify a moderate or bad fit and move on. This process saves wasting everyone's valuable time and efforts. – **Tina**

No matter what, you have to try if you're going to succeed. You can't win or lose a race unless you start. If you don't win your first race, run again. Nobody ever made something of themselves without putting in a little effort.

Perhaps the scariest thing about trying is knowing that you could fail, but failure is just a stepping-stone to success. Winners fail until they succeed; losers quit when they fail. You will fail, and you will fail often, but each time you do, you'll learn something new and gain experience, becoming better prepared for you next shot. After enough trial and error, hard work, and determination, you will succeed. And you will succeed often.

When you do go for it, go 100%. Give it your all and do your best. When you only give a half-committed attempt, it's impossible for you to truly shine. If you half-heartedly go after something, you will expect to fail, and, like a self-fulfilling prophecy, you will—and then all you will have is yourself to blame, knowing you could have tried harder, prepared better, and gone the extra mile. Rather than shoot yourself in the foot, shed your fear, and be your best self.

Take ownership for your actions. You're in control of what you do, so do work you can be proud of. Don't blame others for your failures, but don't dismiss your accomplishments, either. Always give credit where credit is due—to your teammates and to yourself, and take ownership when you make a mistake. Be honest and open, and know that you can always learn from your mistakes and get better. Likewise, you can learn from your successes and continue to improve.

RECAP

So how prepared are you in building up and embracing your success? Answer the following questions about yourself:

1. What makes you who you are? What building blocks have you started with?
2. What have you learned so far in your career? What building blocks have you added?
3. How do you treat others? Have you made valuable connections with your co-workers?
4. How attentive are you? Do people have to prod you for a reply or for a misplaced document, or are you on top of things?
5. How do you keep learning? What new trends or skills do you know?

6. Are you willing to take opportunities and try new things?

PLAYLIST

Enjoy our playlist as you build and embrace success: http://p2q.link/chapter2

CHAPTER 3
MAKING YOURSELF INDISPENSABLE

YOU'VE WORKED HARD. You have chosen your path and built your skills, and you are always looking for ways to improve. Now you have to make sure others recognize your work ethic and expertise. Being your best and making sure others acknowledge it will help you become indispensable at work. How can you make sure you're not just a good employee, but an irreplaceable employee? How can you shine your brightest and work your way up? It starts with visibility.

BE VISIBLE
The key is to be visible. Instead of fading into the background and quietly going about your work, be someone who stands out. By being noticed, you open yourself up to being recruited, promoted, and rewarded. Just as a college athlete needs to be seen by a professional team's recruiter to make their career in sports, you need to be recognized by the right people to make it in your field.

No matter what industry you work in or want to work in, you'll need to be visible. Success largely comes from the right people knowing you, and if you do your best to stand out, you'll have a better chance of getting new opportunities. Speak up!

FINDING YOUR VOICE
During my career, I worked for a large company that believed in internal sales training meetings—and many of them! With a diverse group of individuals that worked for this organization, it was important to share our different backgrounds and knowledge with our peers. Rather than sitting in the back and listening, the people that gave voice to their opinions or asked questions were the most engaged. Acknowledgement

for participation translated into additional opportunities for those that would stand up and be noticed.

Based on that experience, I made sure to always speak up. By sharing my opinion and asking questions, I became a more valuable part of the team. I was able to provide feedback for my team members and have new opportunities to expand my experience and skill sets. **– Tina**

So how do you make yourself visible? Some of it comes from being proactive and ready to volunteer for new projects. Some of it comes from your network. Some of it comes from the quality of your work—and who takes credit for it—and what kind of leadership qualities you possess. Embrace good attention, and do what you can to show your best qualities. With some time and hard work, people will start to notice not just all that you've accomplished, but all the potential you have to do more.

CONFIDENCE IS KEY

In your workplace, you need to be confident in yourself and the work you do. You can let your work speak for itself most of the time, but also make sure you take credit for it. If you come up with an amazing, innovative idea or create an impressive report, you should take credit for your work. When men achieve great things, they typically attribute their success to their innate skills. On the other hand, when women accomplish great things, they tend to attribute that to help from others, good luck, or plenty of hard work—they don't own it the way men do. Are you brushing off your success too much? Be proud of your performance, and don't be shy about owning it!

You should also not be shy about taking your credit in front of others, especially your bosses and co-workers. If a supervisor or co-worker tries to take credit for your great work, politely step in let it be known that you did the work. You don't have to do this in a way that makes the other person look bad or makes you look insecure; there are more subtle tactics that can make it clear. Simply state it as fact. Position it in a way that shows that you did the work, but without throwing your boss under the bus in front of others. Mention that when you did the research, you found out x, y, and z, or you can thank them for liking your work or for agreeing with your idea. Then move on to what's next.

On the flipside, it's also important to give credit where credit is due. If you worked on a project with a team, make it clear that your teammates worked hard and made valuable contributions. Not only will this help your co-workers, but this will also make it clear that you are honest, ethical, and gracious. Your colleagues will be in a position to be respected and get ahead, and so will you.

You don't need to shout out your every success for all to hear. Accepting credit for your work is good, but showing off and droning on about it is not. Rather than make you look successful and competent, it will make you look desperate and narcissistic. Toot your own horn every now and then, but don't do it all the time. Be humble and leave room for others' successes.

BE HELPFUL

It's good to look out for yourself, but it's also important that you look out for your colleagues, too. Remember, you're all on the same team. Helping others is good not just for those you aid, but also for your company overall—and yourself. When others ask you for help, say yes if you have the time and resources. Moreover, when someone needs help, it's always courteous to volunteer.

Helping others makes you more likeable. Your co-workers will appreciate you and have good things to say about you. Supervisors will also likely notice. They'll see you as someone who is competent, able to handle tasks well, and capable of being a leader. It shows that you are proactive and ready for new challenges, not to mention goodhearted.

THE REAL MVP
As an Executive Administrative Assistant, part of my mom's job is setting up meetings in the conference rooms. One day, a new manager approached her to arrange for a meeting. He explained that two of his workers were having disagreements about who was responsible for which tasks, and that he needed to have a meeting with them to work things out.

My mom suggested that he print out the employees' job descriptions, which they would have signed when they were hired; the descriptions clearly outline each position's responsibilities. She also recalled for him her experience from when she was a deli manager at a grocery store, and how she had directed many different types of personalities to work toward a common goal: great customer service. Finally, my mom provided the manager the list of company values for him to refer to during the meeting.

While she was talking to him, the manager was taking notes and was grateful for the advice—especially the idea about the job descriptions. The next day, he told my mom that his meeting had gone well and that he felt that problem was permanently resolved. The manager nominated her for the company's employee of the month (MVP) award, which, thanks to the glowing example he provided in his nomination, my mom won.

Because my mom took the time to listen to this manager's struggles and think of ways to help him, the manager was able to lead his department more effectively, the employees were able to get along better, and my mom's superiors recognized her work in front of the entire company. Everybody won! – **Rachel**

By being helpful, you may also learn some new skills in the process. If your colleague needs help with a task you've never done, you're in the perfect position to learn it. The new skills you acquire will take you far and can prime you for a new position or one that is more senior. In addition to skills, it also teaches you to juggle more tasks and keep them all on track.

HELPING A CO-WORKER, GAINING NEW EXPERIENCE

I had a co-worker whose husband died, and I stepped in to manage her accounts for several months. No one asked me to do this. In fact, someone else had been assigned to cover her accounts. However, within a few short days, I could see that nothing was being done. I simply stepped in and started doing the work that needed to be done.

During the time my co-worker was out, I maintained her accounts and her client relationships.

Taking on her different types of work exposed me to new projects. It was a positive and rewarding growth opportunity for my skills. And yes, for several months, I was crazy busy.

For the company executives and managers, my response demonstrated that I was the type of person who could be relied upon, who would recognize situations that needed to be taken care of, and, most importantly, that I would take immediate action. I gained new types of experience and exposure to new tasks and alternate work styles. It was amazing to make a difference and see the impact I delivered to my co-worker and company. Plus I learned a lot. It was a win-win, all the way around. **– Lynn**

STAYING PROACTIVE

If you want to be indispensable, make it clear that you consider your job indispensable, too. If you prioritize your job and your role within the company, you will become a better—and more essential—employee. Seek out opportunities, and do more than the bare minimum required to finish your work. Seize the chance to impress your colleagues with your skill, adaptability, and dependability.

One of the best ways to propel your career forward is to be proactive. Ask for opportunities, volunteer to work on new projects, and bring forward new ideas. When a new project comes up in your office, instead of quietly hoping you'll be considered, ask your boss directly if you can take it on. If you have an idea that could be valuable to your company, share it with your supervisor. If they like it, you may also be the right person to implement it. Be a go-getter. Not only will it show your passion and commitment, it will also give you a chance to learn new skills. Moreover, it will help you develop leadership qualities that can take you far. You will grow your network and be more visible within the organization.

You can also be proactive in getting a job. Even if a company doesn't have a job listed, it doesn't hurt to inquire about one and offer to help out. During the interviewing process, don't be afraid to regularly email or call your interview contacts for an update on the position. This will show that you truly want the job and are eager to get started. You can also inquire about other ways in which you can help in the meantime. The more proactive and interested you sound, the better your chances of standing out and ultimately getting a job offer.

KEEP ASKING
I have a good friend who wanted to be a journalist in college. Rather than accept an unpaid internship, he landed a job in the mailroom of the city's paper. Every day he introduced himself to the reporters and editors. He asked them if he could ride along when they went out on a story, asked if he could write anything on his time for the paper, volunteered to check out a developing or continuing situation on his way home and report in. Eventually, after cheerfully asking again and again, he was tossed his first small opportunity to write a human interest piece. The paper printed the story, and he had furthered his ambition to be a journalist by getting in the door, staying positive, and asking again and again. – **Tina**

When you are working on different tasks in your company, it's also a good idea to not just make the deadline, but exceed it. There's a common phrase that says you should under promise and over deliver. This means that if you say you'll have a task done by a certain time, try to get it done before then. For example, you can (under) promise to finish a project by Friday, but if you (over) deliver it by Thursday, you exceed expectations. People will recognize that you get things done on time—and sometimes early. This is also great in case you need to make changes or you experience unexpected delays, as you'll have a little extra time available.

When you make promises, though, make sure you're setting a realistic expectation. Always do what you say you're going to do, and only promise what you can reasonably do. Of course, emergencies will come up in life. You can't help it if an earthquake or a broken arm prevents you from completing a task on time. In general, though, you should keep your word. People will respect and trust you more when you do, and you'll become a go-to person that others can rely upon.

Be careful: You don't want to get the phrase backwards. Over promising and under delivering is never the way to go. Always do your best to meet deadlines. If you can't, make sure you let people know in advance with an updated timeline.

Again, make sure you're setting realistic expectations for when you can deliver something.

Another way to be proactive is to never stop learning. Change is constant, and you need to stay on top of the emerging trends in your industry and field. Learn new skills, especially if they may be useful in your career. Maybe it's a good idea to learn a new software tool, coding, or even a new language. It may be something simpler, such as how to use an emerging social tool for your company's marketing purposes. Just because you learned a skill doesn't mean you should stop there; refresh it every now and then. Technology moves rapidly these days, and programs can change quite a bit in a few years or even just months. Think of it this way: Engineers learn a lot in college, but they have to update their knowledge throughout their careers. As new technologies emerge, engineers continue to update their understanding and practices. You should do the same with your skillset, especially if it's something that is continuing to evolve. Otherwise, you risk becoming obsolete with your outdated information.

IMMERSIVE EXPERIENCE
I worked with a fellow that was in international sales who had an opportunity within his corporation to develop sales in Mexico. To prepare for this new position, he took Spanish classes in the US before actually moving in with a family in Mexico to immerse himself in the language. While he was in Mexico, he acquainted himself with Mexican customs, business leadership, and media contacts. He did a lot of pre-networking before taking the sales position, and that really helped.

By the time he began to focus on developing sales in Mexico full time, he was fluent in Spanish as well as Mexican business customs, and he could conduct business on their terms. It was an easier transition for him than somebody coming straight from the United States that a) barely knows the language, and b) doesn't understand the customs or the manner in which business is done. His immersion allowed him to be extremely successful, and he serviced the country of Mexico for the last 10 years of his career. His proactive approach allowed him to be successful from Day One. **– Tina**

Learning skills will help you immensely, but it's also important that you stay up-to-date on your industry and the competition. Read journals and articles relevant to your career, and keep up on emerging trends. Many professional fields have conferences, continuing education opportunities, and certifications. Check them out to expand your horizons and meet new contacts! You can always learn new things and become more valuable within your workplace. This knowledge could help you and your company profoundly, especially if you're ahead of the curve.

INTERPERSONAL PROFESSIONALISM
Pay attention to your attitude when you work with others. You may have heard that people like to be around likeable people; this is true no matter what the situation. Make sure you're likeable and genuine. Try to be confident and have a can-do attitude, even if you feel anything but. This is not to say that you can't have a bad day or be honest about some difficulties or concerns you have—we're all human, after all—but in general, it's better to keep your chin up and stay positive.

On a related note, it's also good to learn how to respond rather than react. When something goes sideways, or someone says something you didn't want to hear, resist the urge to lash out in anger or retort with the first thing that comes to your mind. Those are reactions, and they may be insensitive, harsh, or simply wrong. Take a second to breathe, and then respond. You may even need to take a few minutes or hours. Give yourself a chance to think about the situation clearly and without bias so that you can address it appropriately. You'll say and do things more effectively, won't waste time on unnecessary arguments, and will avoid harming your professional reputation. This maturity and professionalism will also translate to better impressions from your co-workers and supervisors, and possibly more responsibilities.

How you comport yourself is a core foundation as to how you are perceived by your co-workers and supervisors. Maintaining calm assurance demonstrates your leadership, along with reinforcing your abilities to work effectively. In many companies, your performance can be monitored in a myriad of methods, which might include security cameras and examining computer activity and smart device usage. Be conscious to use your time wisely with focus and discipline.

When you have meetings with others, or need to bring up something with a co-worker or boss, be cognizant of their time. It's best to know what you're going to say ahead of time. As we always say, be prepared, be brief, be inspired, and be gone. Get your thoughts together, get to the point, speak candidly, and then let the other respond. You will come off as more professional and prudent.

Being aware of other people's needs and feelings is important to maintaining healthy business relationships, and having good professional relationships makes you valuable to your company. As we said, people like working with likeable people, so having colleagues and peers who are eager to work with you will make you an attractive choice for team leadership positions.

LEADERSHIP QUALITIES

The further you move ahead in your career, the more likely you are to take on some leadership roles. Whether you're in charge of a small team project or become the CEO of a major company, you will need to know how to lead others. It's a skill that develops and evolves over time, and you're likely already taking on some leadership challenges. If you're proactive, you'll take on more leadership roles.

Leaders aren't simply bosses that tell others what to do. Rather, they help a team keep the focus on their end goal and keep everyone on track to reach it. Leaders encourage others and lead by example. What kind of example are you setting? Do you behave the way you think others in your company should behave?

Cultivate the ability to look at projects and tasks from different angles. Shake up your paradigm and consider the perspectives of your co-workers and managers. The old adage of walking a mile in someone else's shoes applies here. It enables you to see the bigger picture, think outside the box, and improve outcomes. Building this skill will help you tremendously on your leadership path.

Leaders also know how to accept feedback from others—no matter their position within the company—and reconsider how they do things. Just because you may be in charge doesn't mean you always know what's best or have all the right ideas. Perhaps another person on your team has a great idea or a different way of seeing things. Your co-workers may offer insight on how you can streamline your approach, pivot, or even change directions. Be open to all of their ideas and feedback. Motivate, encourage, and listen to your team; in turn, they will trust and respect you. Good leaders help a company move forward. The better your leadership skills—even when working with a small team on a small project—the better poised you will be to have a valuable role within the company, and the more likely you are to advance in your career. Learn more about effective leadership practices in *Chapter 13*.

KEEP A GOOD NETWORK

Chapter 7 will cover networking in detail, so we'll keep this brief. The adage says that who you know is even more important than what you know. This may seem unfair, but, in many ways, it is still true. People tend to hire those they already know well, largely because they already know that person's working style, professional ethics, and potential for success.

In your workplace, it's important that in addition to being visible, you take the time to get to know your co-workers. Strike up conversations and catch up on what's going on in your colleagues' lives. Be friendly, genuine, and open while always maintaining your professionalism. Getting to know everyone—from your boss to the janitor—is vital. If they know you and notice you, they will likely value your work more. This will help make you indispensable.

RECAP

Being indispensable starts with being visible, but from there you have to make sure it's the right kind of visibility. For some celebrities, it seems like any attention is good attention, even if they do something deplorable. For the rest of us, it's important that we're showing the best of ourselves, not the worst. Try to exude confidence and self-assurance, help out others when you can, and be proactive with opportunities. Be respectful of others' time and keep your skills and knowledge up-to-date. Learn leadership qualities and grow your network. All of these will help you stay at the forefront of your co-workers' and supervisors' minds. That will make you indispensable.

1. How visible are you? How do you make sure you stand out?

2. Are you confident in yourself and what you do? Do you take credit for your work? Do you give credit to your hardworking colleagues?
3. How much do you help others? What have you learned from helping others?
4. Are you proactive in trying to get new projects? Do you over-deliver on your promises? How do you stay up-to-date on useful skills and industry knowledge?
5. Are you cognizant of others' time? How can you learn how to respond rather than react?
6. What leadership qualities do you possess? Where could you use some improvement?
7. How strong is your network? Is it growing? What do your co-workers and supervisors see in you?

PLAYLIST
The right tunes can motivate you to be proactive and confident. Here are our suggestions: http://p2q.link/chapter3

CHAPTER 4
WORK-LIFE BALANCE & BOUNDARIES

FOLLOWING YOUR DREAMS, working hard, and making yourself an indispensable employee have gotten you to where you are now. Look around and think about what you're proud of and what you still want to achieve. What do you want to accomplish next in your career? And what about your personal life? How does your personal life fit with your professional life? How can you find fulfillment in both? What kinds of hurdles do you have to navigate in finding that balance?

HOW TECHNOLOGY BLURS THE LINES

In old movies and TV shows, people went to their offices to work their 9–5 jobs each day, and when the shift was up, they didn't have to worry about work until the next day. They'd go out or go home and spend time with their family or friends; they'd relax and unwind, and the next morning they were ready to start work all over again.

Today is very different from that fabled time. The lines have blurred more and more over the years, largely thanks to new inventions and consequently shifting norms. For all the amazing gadgets technology has brought us, it has also been a driving factor in changing the way we work. For better or for worse, technology has allowed us to be connected anytime, anywhere.

Watch an old show or period piece, and you'll see businessmen only rarely being interrupted at home by an urgent phone call from work. Now, we can be called, texted, emailed, Facebook messaged, tweeted, video chatted, and in any number of other ways contacted about work-related tasks. And while these primarily occur during working hours, it's all too common to receive these messages well after you've finished your workday.

How many times have you been called just as you're sitting down to watch a late-night movie? How many times has an urgent weekend email from your boss changed your Saturday plans? Even when you're on the other side of the globe enjoying a vacation, a simple press of the button can pull you right back into work mode, interrupting your beachside relaxation for an urgent inquiry.

If your boss *expects* you to be reachable at all hours, as over 65% of employers seem to, you may feel that you have little choice in the matter.[1] It might be reasonable to expect employees to be reachable in case of an absolute emergency, but this should be used as rarely as it used to be to call an employee's home phone. As technologies have made it easier to reach anyone at any time, it is important for workers and managers alike to set and recognize boundaries.

The blame isn't entirely on others encroaching on your deserved time off. Many of us are guilty ourselves. We feel the need to check that work email before going to bed. We prioritize completing small work tasks after hours and even on weekends, knowing it's easy to just get online and get it done really fast. We send messages to our co-workers asking about a needed document.

Email, social media, texting, apps, and good old-fashioned phone calls have made us more reachable and have reduced that barrier between work life and personal life. We're constantly connected no matter where we are. For all the convenience and streamlining technology allows, it also tips that work-life balance out of whack. The work side weighs a little heavier now, and it can be difficult to remove some of that pressure. While it can allow flexibility, the more we blur the lines, the more it's normalized—but it's not healthy, and it can lead to burnout.

So how do you unplug after work so you can enjoy your time off? Should you disconnect? While it may be impossible to completely disconnect, it may be helpful to limit how reachable you are. Limit how many times you check your work email at night, or keep your work email off your smartphone. Put your phone away for an hour or two. Spend some time away from the computer and just focus on what you're doing and who you're with. Try to limit how immediately reachable you are so that you have some time for yourself.

---

1   http://workplacetrends.com/the-2015-workplace-flexibility-study/

HOW WORKING AT HOME FURTHER BLURS THE LINES

A few decades ago, it was virtually unheard of to work from your home. Unless your business was based in your house, you had to go to a workplace and put in your eight (or more) hours. Over the years, however, more and more people are telecommuting full- or part-time. This is largely thanks to technological advancements and evolving office cultures. As described in the above section, we can communicate with each other in any number of ways involving written messages, verbal talks, and video chatting. We can send each other any document we're working on and look up anything we need to know from our personal computer.

As of 2016, 20-25% of people work from home at least part time,[2] and 2.8% of workers telecommute at least half of the time.[3] The number of people who would like to telework at least part time is much higher—up to 90%. Telecommuting is rapidly growing in popularity among businesses and workers alike, a trend that's expected to continue.

Working from home may sound like a dream. You can avoid rush hour traffic, wear comfortable clothes, and eat a healthy, home-cooked meal for lunch. Your schedule can be flexible, and even some household chores can be squeezed in during breaks. However, there are some downsides to working from home. In the context of traditional office jobs, teleworkers tend to be less visible—out of sight, out of mind. Even if these workers do all their work well and on time, their superiors and peers might view them as less committed and less valuable overall. If you want to telecommute, you will need to work harder to stay visible.

There is another dark side to teleworking. It provides freedom... but maybe too much freedom. It can be easy to get distracted for a few minutes—or hours—as you run errands, pay bills, surf the web, and walk the dog. Because your work still needs to be done, you may have to work later into the evening than you otherwise would. Your work time and personal time can start to blend together. For some people, telecommuting creates a much better work-life balance. For others, the softened boundaries mean a more unified

---

2   http://www.pcmaconvene.org/features/cmp-series/how-meeting-planners-are-maximizing-the-benefits-of-telecommuting/
3   http://globalworkplaceanalytics.com/telecommuting-statistics

schedule in which work and personal tasks move into each other's time.

If you work from home—whether full-time or just one day per week—you may want to set up your own boundaries. Perhaps you don't allow yourself to do any household chores until after lunch. Maybe you don't run errands until you're finished working for the day. It can help to make a strict schedule and treat your job like a traditional office job. It might also work for you to create a space in your home that is specifically for work: Working in a home office can put you in the right mindset and prevent against distractions.

HOME-LIFE IMBALANCE
When I first started telecommuting and working offsite, it coincided with a challenging organizational shift at our corporation. I easily fell into the trap of not only working a 10-hour day, but working well into the night. Having a dedicated home office made it easy for me to work and work and work. It took me years to break the bad habits I developed regarding work-life balance. Now I have set work hours every day, and I stick with them except in unusual and temporary situations. It's exactly how I would work if I were to go into an office.
– Lynn

If you have the opportunity to work from home, take a hard look at your potential work environment. Does it foster your ability to remain focused and successful? You need to know going in that working from home requires strict discipline and diligence. Be honest with yourself because it's not for everyone. You may prefer the structure and camaraderie of the workplace environment in order to be effective and productive.

For many, working from home is a luxury, and if you become used to it, it can be more fulfilling and efficient than working onsite. If you're able to juggle your home and work duties, more power to you! But if you have difficulty staying focused, or feel that it's causing you to work later into the night than you'd prefer, re-evaluate and enforce your own boundaries.

THE NEED TO SET BOUNDARIES
Thanks in part to our connectivity, it's very easy to work during evenings, weekends, and even vacations these days. Many of

us have muddied distinctions within our communications and social channels. We're all accustomed to being just a message or email away from a colleague, and people have started to blur the lines between work time and personal time. Nearly all of us are guilty of this—but are we happy with this setup?

When you get an email late in the day, responding to it right away signals to your co-workers that you're still willing and able to work at that time. If you're always replying, whether it's an evening or a weekend, you're giving your colleagues permission to continue to send you work even when it should be your time off. You're making your own work schedule, and making it very clear that you're ready to work at any time of day.

When you give your colleagues this permission, they are more likely to take advantage of the opportunity. They will send you an email after dinner more frequently, and then expect you to respond to it right away. Eventually, this will become a source of resentment and stress for you as you bend over backwards to get things done last minute, interrupting your personal time.

It is important that you set boundaries with your colleagues and supervisors. Do not respond to messages or calls after a certain time of day or on weekends. Make it clear that you're truly out of the office. Soon enough they'll understand that you do not work at those times. If they don't, you may have to explain so directly.

Of course, there are exceptions to this rule. If there is an emergency, it would be best if you do reply. If your co-worker is hounding you, sending you multiple messages or using various platforms in an effort to reach you, reply. If it's not an emergency, you can at least respond by saying you will address it the next morning. They'll feel that you have heard them and responded, but you're also still confirming your boundaries about a non-crisis.

It's not realistic to have zero tolerance; emergencies and urgent issues will come up, and it's important to be responsive in crisis situations. Otherwise, be adamant about your boundaries. This will help you keep your work life separate from your personal life. Most people will be reasonable if they know what to expect from you. On the other hand, if you do find yourself doing extra work, make sure you get recognition and compensation for it. The extra work you do should not go unnoticed.

LYNN'S CHECKLIST
- ☑ Put your mobile devices on silent.
- ☑ Close your email.
- ☑ If you do check your emails, don't respond until work hours. If you are compelled to answer, say that you will reply during work hours (unless it's a true crisis).
- ☑ If you're catching up on work or getting ahead, schedule your emails to send during work hours.
- ☑ If your work load consistently requires that you work after hours or on weekends,
    - ☑ Examine your tasks and methods for ways to streamline them,
    - ☑ Keep track of the time you spend on tasks, and
    - ☑ Talk to your supervisor about how to dial back your responsibilities to fit within a normal work week.

DON'T BRING WORK HOME WITH YOU

Although technology continues to expand and invade our personal lives, we have brought it home with us for decades. Work is such a major part of our lives that it's natural that we think and talk about it while we're not working. Be careful, though, because it can become a problem when you let work pervade your whole life.

Do you find that you get home from a stressful day at work only to talk on and on about it to your family or friends? Does work continue to linger in your mind throughout the evening or weekend? Don't let your job take over your life.

Limit how much you vent about work to your family or friends. It's okay to talk about it for 10 minutes when you get home, but don't let it stretch too much beyond that on most days. It can make you feel like you're still working and can leave you feeling stressed or drained, not to mention the way it might make your friends and family feel. You need to be able to clear your mind and think about other things when you're not working. It will help you recharge and re-center.

If it's hard for you to go from work mode to personal mode, it can help to find some kind of transition activity between the two. On your way home from work, stop at the gym to exercise for an hour. Not only will it clear your mind, it will also help you physically get the stress out. You can also meet up with friends for a cup of coffee after leaving the office. Do something that you enjoy and that will allow you to clear your mind.

PERSONAL LIFE VS. PROFESSIONAL LIFE
Bringing work home with you is acceptable in moderation, but it's good to limit how much you think and talk about it when you're not working. What about if we turn things around? How much should your personal life seep into your professional life?

Back in the 1970s and '80s, when Tina and Lynn were just starting in the work force, women were generally expected to maintain complete professionalism. Tina, in particular, responded by becoming very compartmentalized. She didn't want her two worlds to blend together much. Although she was friendly and open with her colleagues and clients, she avoided talking about personal matters. Over the years, though, she's found value in being less rigid in her separation of work life and personal life. She is more comfortable sharing both halves of herself.

> ### A SECRET DIVORCE
> *I was really of the mindset that it was not okay to share about your personal life at work. I felt that it would give people a certain advantage over you if they knew your personal information.*
>
> *I was experiencing a rather traumatic divorce which, unfortunately, demanded that I notify security for my safety. I never alerted the people with whom I worked... again, thinking that work is work and personal is personal. Great—until the day security had to come up to my office to alert me to a situation. Now everyone in the office knew and felt betrayed that I hadn't shared this with them. I learned a valuable lesson and now know that it is okay to share a bit.* **– Tina**

Nowadays, it seems that most people are much more open than they were in previous decades. Perhaps it's partially due to social media. Millennials have grown up with MySpace, Facebook, Twitter, Instagram, and now Snapchat, and many are used to sharing some of their most personal moments for all their friends and followers to see. Whether it's a photo of their engagement or wedding, song lyrics that mean the world to them, or a quick video of them having good times with their friends, millennials have become very comfortable with letting others see your day-to-day lives through their eyes.

It's important to be aware of how your social posts and activities can influence the perception by your co-workers and supervisors. In fact, your public profiles can be accessed by anyone and everyone. Keeping your personal and professional channels separate will help you maintain your balance. And please, think before you post!

When it comes to work, how much of your personal life should come with you to the office? How comfortable are you talking about personal matters with co-workers? And even if you are comfortable, are your co-workers comfortable hearing about it? At this point, it is normal and even expected that you'll talk about your personal life at least to some degree. People tend to be more open and relaxed now, and we understand that everyone is a whole person with a life outside of work. Don't be afraid to show that, if in a professional manner. Still, be mindful of the stories you choose to share and how they might affect your colleagues' perception of you; put your best foot forward.

You should be a whole person. It's great to be ambitious and focused on your career, but do you want that to be your whole life? Maybe you want to balance out your excellent career and work ethic with some close friendships and relationships, hobbies you're passionate about, or volunteer work. On the other hand, you may feel that love and family are your #1 priorities, but do you also work, volunteer, or have hobbies?

DEFINED BY WORK
There was a time in my life where I was absolutely defined by my work. If I didn't have my work, what was I? That was a difficult lesson to learn, and one which I wish I had learned earlier. Someone says, "Tell me something about yourself," and I would respond with my job title and job-related accomplishments. I have rethought my response to the question and now ask for context—do you mean in work or outside of work? I might start out with sharing that I am the eldest of three and enjoy music and crossword puzzles. Then let the conversation move on from there! **– Tina**

It's great to have a specific passion, but you don't want to be 100% defined by one thing. If something goes wrong, you may feel your sense of self weaken as you try to regain your footing. Let yourself be a whole person with diverse interests. Even if you just bump it up to two things you fully value, at least you won't be dependent on one aspect of your life bringing you all your happiness and sense of fulfillment.

DOING IT ALL

When women enter the workplace, they are often met with some added layers of difficulty that men typically do not face. Women have traditionally been the caretakers who keep the home clean and the children well-behaved; men were the breadwinners who focused primarily on their careers. Over the last half century, though, there has been the growing need for a change not just in the workforce, but also in homes.

Women have made great strides in work, yet there's still plenty of progress to be made. The home has seen less improvement, with women who work full-time still taking on the bulk of household chores and childcare.[4,5] As women continue to advance in their careers, it's important that men take on an equal share of housework. Luckily, younger generations of men and women seem to be much more open to work and home equality.[6] We no longer just have stay-at-home moms with breadwinner husbands; we also have stay-at-home dads with breadwinner wives.[7] The playing fields are slowly but surely becoming more equal. Gender norms are finally starting to change.

For women, there is a pressure to "do it all." Many women want to be successful in their careers, but many also want to have great family lives with clean homes, loving spouses, and happy children. Most women also want to have fulfilling personal lives, in which they have time to go to the gym, meet up with friends, and spend some alone time curled up with a book or musical instrument. That's a lot to juggle.

Some people say that "doing it all" is a myth and "having it all" is impossible. How can you do *everything*? One of the first

---

4   http://www.bls.gov/news.release/atus.nr0.htm
5   http://www.pewsocialtrends.org/2013/03/14/modern-parenthood-roles-of-moms-and-dads-converge-as-they-balance-work-and-family/
6   Ibid.
7   http://www.bloomberg.com/news/articles/2012-01-04/behind-every-great-woman

things to accept is everything can't and won't be perfect all the time. Even if you have your happy family and amazing job, there will be struggles and stresses, and you will occasionally need to take a step back and reprioritize things.

It's important that you have others to help you—and that you're willing to accept their help. If you have a spouse or partner, make sure they're helping out. Let them take over some of the household chores, or ask them to take charge of certain aspects of childcare (or pet care). Be able to have honest conversations so that neither one of you feels like you're doing too much or the other person is not doing enough.

The more help and support you have, the easier it will be to manage everything. Remember, your support doesn't have to come from a romantic partner; it can also come from siblings, friends, and family members.

Be ambitious and set goals for yourself. Don't beat yourself up if you simply can't juggle everything at once. Set realistic goals, and maybe spread them out so that you can focus on one goal at a time. If you want to learn a new language but also want to join a club—but don't have enough time for both—perhaps you can try doing one first before adding the other. Give yourself the time and flexibility you need, and accept that you're doing your best. Be happy that you have and do the things you want, and know that things won't always be perfect and that's okay.

Work and life can feel like a balancing act, and it's okay to do things in the way that work best for you. Just do whatever feels right for you.

RECAP

Work-life balance is hard to achieve, and even harder given the ways technology has changed our availability and expectations. With so many things pulling us in so many directions, it's important that you stay true to yourself. Set your own goals and make boundaries for yourself. You don't have to work every night and every weekend; you don't have to do it all to be successful. Make sure you feel fulfilled professionally as well as personally, and don't let one take away from the other. It may be a struggle to find your balance at first, but it's worth it in the long run. Here are some questions to get you thinking about your own work-life balance:

1. How do social media, email, video chatting, and phones affect your off time? How do you unplug after work so that you can enjoy some personal time?
2. Does telecommuting help you find more work-life balance, or do you find your personal and professional lives blending? How do you deal with all that working from home comes with?
3. Do you feel like your co-workers take advantage of your time? How have you set boundaries for when you respond to messages?
4. Do you bring work home with you? How do you transition between work mode and personal mode?
5. What are your goals in work and in your personal life? Do you feel pressure to do it all? How will you deal with that pressure?

PLAYLIST
Find your balance with the help of our playlist at: http://p2q.link/chapter4

CHAPTER 5
TIME MANAGEMENT

SOMETIMES IT FEELS like there isn't enough time in a day for your never-ending to-do list. It seems like everyone is always busy, whether it's with work, chores, or outside activities and semi-neglected hobbies. With all that's going on, it's important to know how to manage time effectively. The more wisely you use your time, the more time you will have for other fulfilling activities, and you'll also probably feel less stress.

How well do you manage your time? What time management style works best for you? Here are some tips that can help you take control of your time.

EVERYONE IS DIFFERENT

We all work differently and have ways of doing things that may work for us but not others. It might take a few attempts to figure out what is best for you, but once you've found it, don't worry if it doesn't line up with how your best friend or colleague manages her time.

Some people are very rigid with how they manage their time. They may keep a very detailed, strict calendar and have their whole day planned out front to back. These people may use numerous tools and resources to manage their time (more on this later) and might work best with a clear to-do list mapping out their weekly tasks.

Other people are looser or more flexible with their time management. They might shy away from committing to a schedule, instead preferring to go with the flow each day. They might be more productive without stifling time constraints and firm work plans.

As you navigate your working style, try to pay attention to how you manage your time. Do you like how you do things? Do you wish you were more organized and more aware of your deadlines or appointments? Or do you feel confined and like you need more freedom to work flexibly? Do you often lose track of what needs to be done? Are you frequently late or missing appointments? Do you have a clear idea of your priorities and devote your attention to the things that are most impactful first?

Different people work better with contrasting systems of time management. Whatever style feels best to you, make sure that you're productive and not having a negative impact on others' schedules.

KNOW YOURSELF

The key to time management is knowing yourself. Ask yourself, "What motivates me?" Understanding your motivations will assist you in achieving better time management. Self-awareness in your work habits and preferences go hand-in-hand with enthusiasm for tasks you like and exasperation with responsibilities you don't. For the jobs you dread, you may find yourself delaying them or welcoming interruptions. Knowing yourself also means identifying how the time of day, week, or season may influence your mindset.

Set aside some time to consider when and how you work best and are the most effective. Ask some close friends and/or peers to weigh in with what they've observed about you. You may even want to keep a record for a week or a month to track when you are the most efficient and motivated. Use your new knowledge to make conscious adjustments that will be more effective and allow you to better manage your time.

If you have a hard time identifying what works well for you, you can start by figuring out what you *don't* like. As you note environments that stifle your work—perhaps it's having a lot of noise or having too much clutter on your desk—you will be able to zero in on the environment that is most supportive of your work. The same goes for communication; as you notice forms you are uncomfortable with, you will find what works best for you.

In both your office space and your communication, you likely won't be able to create the perfect situation. While a work paradise might be elusive, however, you can make small adjustments to boost your efficiency. If having people talking around you is disruptive, but you work in a cubicle where such conversations are unavoidable, see if you can wear headphones or use a fan to create white noise.

As you discover how you work best, you will be able to work more efficiently and manage your time more effectively.

Knowing how to cut out distractions and keep yourself motivated is the best way to keep moving forward with your tasks. This is why the first step to time management is always knowing yourself and your preferences.

MAKE A PLAN

Regardless of what style you choose, it's usually a good idea to have a plan or a clear goal in mind. What kind of plan you need will depend on the type of job you have and the work you need to complete that day or week.

For many, a good place to start is with a prioritized to-do list. Children often learn about this in grade school as a way to manage their increasing amount of homework. They are often given a school planner listing the days of the week and are encouraged to write down what homework they need to do that day, when upcoming exams will be held, and when they have other activities with which they are involved. Planners are helpful throughout grade school and college, and they can continue to aid in keeping up with work and life tasks.

Whether you write a to-do list for the day or for the week, it can help you remember to complete certain errands and projects on time. Some people use one to-do list for everything, while others may prefer to use separate to-do lists for work and for their home.

To-do lists don't have to be in physical planners or on random sticky notes; they can also be on your computer, smart phone, or tablet. There are many apps available with reminders, calendars, and organizers to help you stay on-task throughout the day. Many of these will pop up and remind you what time you need to perform these tasks. Whether it's a reminder to pay your credit card bill or to finish your monthly job report, they can help keep even the busiest people up to speed.

When you start a new project, it's usually a great idea to plan out what needs to be done and when. Prioritize tasks to stay on track and meet your deadlines. Create an outline or schedule and figure out how the work will need to be done, who will complete what tasks, and what additional information or tools you'll need.

For example, this chapter didn't just pour out of us in a sudden inspiration-fueled burst of activity. Rather, we started by making a list of what kinds of topics we wanted to discuss. Then we reorganized that list of ideas into a specific outline, which became the bones of this chapter. We knew what sections we had to write, filled each one in, and went back for editing and revisions. This chapter started with a clear plan—in fact, the whole book did—and that plan helped in making the work process focused and efficient.

What needs to get done with your next project? Do you need to complete certain tasks before you can tackle others? How long will each task take? List everything you can and try to be specific. It's also good to plan for extra time, even if you're sure something only takes X number of minutes. Things can go sideways, and it's best to be prepared for unexpected changes or delays.

Having a clear plan will help you work efficiently, avoid mistakes, and minimize the need to redo work. It helps to know where you're going before you take the first step, and knowing what to expect will make the whole process easier.

BE COGNIZANT OF OTHERS' TIME

Managing your own time is vital, but it's also important that you keep others' schedules in mind, too. This is true of life in general, but is especially so in a work environment. There's always plenty to do, and, more often than not, the work others can complete will depend on the work you do and your timeliness.

As a general rule of thumb, you should always try to respond to people quickly. When you receive an email, respond right away if you have the answer or document ready. If you anticipate a delay before you can address their inquiry, let them know when you plan to reply. It's a good idea to respond within one business day, but sooner is better.

Also be cognizant of when you respond to co-workers, and be respectful of their personal time. We described issues of work-life balance in the previous chapter, including the downside of always being available thanks to technology. That message bears repeating here. Be mindful of when people end their workdays. Don't send them work emails or call them with urgent requests when they're trying to enjoy their evening. Likewise, avoid sending emails on weekends. It may seem harmless, but many people get buzzing notifications on their smart phone each time a work email appears in their inbox. This can be stressful and distracting from an otherwise enjoyable weekend.

THE NEED TO RESPOND
I am a little like Pavlov's dogs in that I hear a beep, and I immediately feel like I have to stop what I'm doing and look and respond to the message. But it's not always necessary.

It's a matter of time management for business communications. I strongly believe that there are general hours in a day in which it's appropriate to respond to people or to be sending emails out, and there are times when it's not okay. Just as I don't call somebody at 10 o'clock at night, I don't email someone at 10 o'clock at night. What I try to do is put a timer on the email and send things out first thing in the morning. I don't care if I'm working on it all night; I'm not going to send it at one or two in the morning. **– Tina**

In some positions, when you work is up to you. Perhaps you're a night owl who feels especially motivated or creative after 7:00 PM. It's acceptable to work at that time, but don't expect others to be on that schedule. You can write up your emails and set a reminder to send them for later, or even schedule them to automatically send at a more reasonable hour. Every work culture has its own schedule and norms, but when you step outside that timeframe, make sure you're not dragging others with you unwillingly.

Keeping track of co-workers' schedules doesn't just apply to phone calls, emails, and social media messages. It is also important when working on projects or other tasks that are relevant for your colleagues. Usually, when a team works on a project, things need to be accomplished in a particular order or by specific deadlines to keep things are track. Certain tasks are interrelated and need to be completed before others can begin. When you're working with others, make sure you're not the one holding up the project. If a team member needs your research, outline, or document done before she can complete her part, make sure you have it to her on time. If you find that won't be possible, let her know of the delay up front and provide a new ETA. Keep delays to an absolute minimum so the whole team can work together efficiently.

DITCHING PROCRASTINATION
One hurdle many people face is procrastination. It's natural to

want to put things off and work on easier or more enjoyable tasks first. There will be projects and tasks that you won't like as much, and you may feel the urge to delay them until later. Nonetheless, do what you can to resist this urge. Procrastination is a slippery slope, and it's better to just finish the task before the delay goes too far.

For some people, it's easiest to simply do things right away. When you get an assignment, tackle it immediately. If you do, you'll be ready for the next project that comes your way. However, this will not always be feasible. Workers aren't usually sitting around waiting for something to do; on the contrary, it seems that most people have too much to do! Deadlines for other projects will likely take precedence over newer tasks that are due later. Likewise, you won't always be able to work on a new project right away.

That's when it will end up on your to-do list. When you're making your reminders, to-do list, or calendar notifications, the best way to avoid procrastination is to schedule the dreaded tasks first. What's the one assignment you don't want to do? Tackle it first. Once you get it done, you'll feel less stress, more accomplished, and ready to work on the other tasks you might enjoy more.

When there's an undesirable project looming ahead of you, the longer you put it off, the more stress it builds in you. You may become more and more conscious of it and feel growing guilt in continually delaying it. Procrastination doesn't help you, so do what you can to keep things moving. Get everything done in order and on time, and feel good when you check those things off your list.

SIDE-STEP DISTRACTIONS

Having a plan is great, but what about distractions and interruptions that may slow you down? While there have always been distractions, it seems to be more prevalent now than it was just a few decades ago. No matter where you work, there will be something that takes away from your concentration and efficiency.

At the office, you may encounter talkative co-workers, unproductive meetings, and unexpected minor assignments from your colleagues. If you work at home, you may get sidetracked by pending household chores, family members or roommates making noise, needy pets, or even just a ringing doorbell. You'll also likely face some of the usual office distractions, albeit to a lesser degree.

> **BEING PRESENT**
> *There are two things that sidetrack me during the day: emails and phone calls. I can have a calendar that shows me where I'm supposed to be at a particular time, but it doesn't tell me how to manage the scores of emails that come in from my six different email accounts or my telephone calls that can come in from four different lines. I get so darn sidetracked that I don't end up doing what I need to be doing, or I end up being late to an appointment.*
>
> *What I've learned to do now is to be present with one telephone and send all others to voicemail, and to be present with one or two emails, and everything else I will look at when I have an opportunity.* – **Tina**

Whether you work at home or at the office, we also have one shinier distraction machine: the internet. Social media, random articles, cat videos, and more can all call out for your attention. Email pings and message chimes will eat into your concentration. Even things like solitaire games and some good tunes are just a click away from drawing your attention away from your work.

It's a lot to deal with, but there are ways to limit these distractions. You may want to start by finding a method that allows you to focus on the task at hand while minimizing outside influences. Perhaps you need to drown out noise. You could use headphones to cover sounds of voices and barks with music; headphones also indicate to others that you are busy and not interested in talking. You may want to close your office door if possible. It's also a good idea to put your phone on silent, or even put it away so it's out of sight.

Those of you with a penchant for surfing the internet or checking your social media accounts may want to look into website blockers. You may want to set up a blocker that thwarts your attempts to get onto Facebook or YouTube. Maybe you need to turn off your internet access altogether for a few hours. There are plenty of tools available to help you.

Pick a method that works for you. Everyone has different preferences and needs, so make sure you know what you're trying to ignore and how you respond to your environment. Also keep in mind what you still need to be aware of. You can't ignore every distraction, but you can minimize many of them.

As we discussed in *Chapter 3*, being completely present and focused on your tasks at work will not go unnoticed by your supervisors. Their perception of your job performance encompasses your diligence and attentiveness. Your daily activities, the websites you visit, the session duration, email interaction, and call logs, can all be monitored to evaluate your performance. This monitoring includes all company devices and equipment, and your activities after normal business hours. How you manage and spend your time will directly impact your success.

HOW TO WORK FROM HOME

We touched on how to work from home in *Chapter 4*, but it is also useful to address it within a time management context. Like it or not, working from home comes with some very different challenges and opportunities than traditional onsite work. How can you manage time efficiently when you're your own supervisor?

If it's feasible where you live, it can help to have a specific area of your home dedicated just to work. If you have an extra bedroom or a den, turn it into an office. When you're in that room, only do work-related tasks. It's best to avoid turning it into a multi-purpose room. If your brain associates that space with working, it will be easier to concentrate when you're there. You'll be able to mentally go to work even though you're still in your home. You can take it a step further and put on business clothes. Pajamas may be more comfortable, but they might not get your head in the right space for working.

During your work time, act as if you're truly at the office. Try not to mix up household chores with your work assignments. Leave errands and chores for later in the day. Create a schedule that creates separate times to focus on work and then shift your attention to home and personal matters. How you construct your day is up to you, but you should try to keep your work and personal times distinct.

It can be difficult to not work at all hours of the day. Pay attention and stay focused to maintain a disciplined routine. When you work from home, it's as if you never really leave your worksite. Do your best to give yourself an end time each day so you're no longer sending work emails while watching a late-night show. It's not healthy or efficient. This is part of why it's so important to designate one area of your home for work: It helps to separate your work and personal life a bit so that you can enjoy time for yourself.

ALL DRESSED UP WITH NOWHERE TO GO

About twelve years ago, I began representing a company that did not want to open a satellite office, so I was supported to set-up an office in my home. Computer, desk, bookcases—all the comforts of a corporate space turning a spare bedroom into my "office." I actually placed a name plate next to the door as a reminder for anyone present that through these doors is my workplace, which also allowed me to "leave" the office when I shut the door. I would get up every morning and get dressed for work: full make-up, suit, and shoes. For me, it set the professional tone of my day and actions, even if only through a series of telephone interactions. I maintain that standard to this day, and although I have an actual off-site office, I keep a presence at my home office for those days I do not have to physically drive in. I have the flexibility to conduct meetings on– or off-site, and it balances quite well for me. **– Tina**

WHAT TO DO IF YOU'RE OVERWHELMED

If you find yourself overwhelmed with all your work assignments—and even with household and personal tasks—you may need to take a step back to reevaluate your situation and prioritize your needs. You might need to reconsider your approach to time management or start using some helpful tools. On the other hand, you may simply have too much on your plate. Here are some ways you can streamline your time.

SURVIVING MARS

There have been many times that I've had too much on my plate; it would have been easy to succumb to feelings of being overwhelmed. It's vital to not let those feelings take over. Rather like the lead character in The Martian, *you have to plan, prioritize, and "solve one problem at a time."*

> *While I've never been in a life or death situation on Mars, the workload did seem like the makings of a perfect storm. To avoid the fallout, I first created an overview of my projects and timelines. Within an hour, I had a solid foundation on which to build a plan and prioritize tasks. The time spent to organize my projects and deadlines has always been the key to not just getting through these intense periods, but empowering myself and succeeding.* **– Lynn**

Do you use to-do lists, planners, digital reminders, or calendars? Perhaps a computer spreadsheet or a physical whiteboard is more your style? Whether you like traditional pen and paper, computer programs, or phone apps, there are plenty of tools available to help you keep track of everything you have going on. Write down what needs doing and when it's due. Outline how projects should be organized, who should complete each task, and the best programs to use to maintain efficiency. Having everything in your head may work for a while, but eventually there will be too much for you to remember—and it will leave your co-workers without guidance if you're out of the office. It's best to get in the habit of having everything written down and mapped out.

Do you delegate when possible? Sometimes it can feel like you have to get everything done yourself, but that can leave you burnt out and even doing things more poorly due to your exhaustion. See if there are colleagues that may be a good fit for certain tasks and ask them to take them on. Management and more experienced workers in particular are good at finding the right people to whom to delegate tasks. If you're a lower-level employee, it may not be possible to delegate, but you might find that a co-worker has some extra time on their hands.

When you're working through a project, it's important that you're open to immediate process improvement. You may not be using your time as efficiently as possible. Just because you started a certain way doesn't mean it makes sense to complete the whole project that way; you may find that there are shortcuts that can speed up the process. Change how you work as you go so that you waste as little time as possible.

Ask your peers about the tools they use. If nothing helps and you find that you're always busy and running behind, you may have too much that you're responsible for—and there's no shame in that! There are many reasons why this could be the case, but at that point, you'll have to see what you can eliminate. You may need to talk to your boss to reevaluate your workload. You may need to ask a family member or roommate to take on one of your chores. Find ways that you can alleviate your workload and focus on what matters most.

MAKE TIME FOR YOURSELF

So far we've been talking about how to make the most of your time at work, but there's one important thing to remember: You also need to make time for yourself. We are not machines, and we can't just focus all our time and attention on work. We also need a chance to relax and recharge. When you're planning out your day or week, remember to leave some free time for yourself. You can also schedule in some specific activities you want to do.

Whatever you do in your "you" time should be something you enjoy. It also helps if it's something that makes you feel rejuvenated or inspired. Try meditation, yoga, exercising, reading, or another activity that you like. When you do these activities, try to clear your mind of any work stress or anxiety you might have. Just focus on yourself and what you're doing in that moment. You will unwind, de-stress, and find yourself more prepared for the rest of your day.

RECAP

Time management is an important part of working efficiently and keeping your life running smoothly. For some people, time management skills come naturally. For others, these are skills you will need to develop. Everyone works differently, and you should stay honest with yourself as you figure out what's best for you. Just remember these tips on how you can keep yourself on track and on time. Here are some questions to help you fine tune your time management:

1. What is your time management style? Is it effective for you? If not, how can you improve your time management?
2. How do you plan out what you have to do? What tools are most useful for you?
3. Do you keep others' schedules in mind when sending messages or working on tasks?

4. Is procrastination a problem for you? How do you combat it?
5. What kinds of distractions do you face? How do you limit distractions?
6. What challenges do you find in working from home? How do you overcome these challenges?
7. Do you ever feel overwhelmed by your workload? Have you found ways to improve your time management? Do you have too much on your plate?
8. Do you make time for yourself? How do you like to spend your alone time?

PLAYLIST
Music is a great way to find your perfect timing. We have just the playlist: http://p2q.link/chapter5

CHAPTER 6
STRESS MANAGEMENT

Everyone deals with stress. We can try to avoid or minimize stressful situations, but some things will always be unavoidable. Each of us handles and expresses stress differently, and it's important that we are managing it in a healthy, constructive way. How you address stress will have far-reaching impacts on your personal and professional life. Here are some tools to consider for managing stress in your life.

SOURCES OF STRESS

Stress can come from a myriad of sources and will vary in how strongly it affects you—some kinds of stress will be easier for you to manage than others. It will be helpful to be prepared for the types of stress you are likely to encounter.

There are two main categories that stress falls under: the stress that comes from outside sources and the stress we put on ourselves. In general, stress comes from uncertainty and things that we have little control over. These can be major, important events or many little struggles that add up. When circumstances are adverse or demanding, that's when stress comes out in full force. We feel anxiety because we care about what happens but feel there's little we can do to secure the outcome. It can feel like things are up in the air and all we can do is wait for the conclusion.

One of the most common causes of stress is money (especially the lack thereof). Money is the ticket to paying for housing, food, school, healthcare, travel, and nearly every other material or non-material necessity in life. Another top source of stress is your job or job search. Today's job market is tough, and finding employment can be slow and discouraging. It's stressful, especially when you need a paycheck for your rent. Once you are hired, stress will likely shift a bit. Even the most enjoyable, fulfilling jobs can be rife with deadlines, shifting office politics, worries about your performance, and how it balances out with your personal life. For most people, money and employment are significant concerns they must navigate continuously.

Stress also frequently comes from people. You may have concern for your romantic partner, parents, children, siblings, or other close family members. Issues with friends, co-workers, neighbors, and strangers can cause you to worry. If a loved one is sick, or if you haven't heard from someone in a while, or if there are arguments or fights between you and someone you care about, you will likely feel a lot of stress.

And you may not know it, but you probably put a lot of stress on yourself. Having high expectations for yourself can motivate you to achieve great success, but it can also put too much weight on your shoulders, especially if you misstep or face a delay. So much stress comes from nagging worries in our own heads, worst-case scenarios and self-deprecating thoughts turning adrenaline into stress. We don't mean to stress ourselves out, and yet sometimes we can be our own worst enemies. It can be hard to accept where we are now.

Where does your stress come from? How much of it is from uncontrollable outside sources... and how much of it comes from pressure you put on yourself? Are your worries well-founded, or are you interpreting things negatively? Challenge these thoughts and make sure you are not habitually adding stress where it is not necessary or helpful in achieving your goals.

MINIMIZE STRESSFUL SITUATIONS

If you know where your stress comes from, you have a better chance of learning how to minimize or avoid it. Think about whether you can eliminate your sources of stress entirely, or at least greatly reduce them, and then plan out a path to get there.

Time management (discussed in *Chapter 5*) is closely related to stress management. A lot of stress comes from the sense that you're always running out of time—when there aren't enough hours in the day to get everything done, you're always late, or you don't make time for yourself each day.

"NO" ISN'T FOREVER
I have a bad habit of double– or triple-booking myself—I will fit in as many meetings, telephone calls, and conversations as I possibly can in a day, and this causes a lot of stressful situations. When I overbook myself, I think that I'm doing the right thing because

I'm giving time to other people, but what I'm really doing is cheating people out of time because I'm always running a little behind or I'm thinking about the next place I need to be, and I'm not fully present. I need to remember sometimes that "no" isn't "no forever." It can just be giving yourself some breathing room in things that you're doing and being able to absorb.

Being prompt is showing respect for another's time. Unfortunately, my bad habit of running late, regardless of the reason, doesn't coincide with my value. Therefore, I am constantly at odds with myself! I continue to strive for improvement in this area— allowing a 15-minute adaptable time in the schedule. No matter the circumstance, though, if you are running behind, always notify the person and allow them the courtesy to reschedule. **– Tina**

Learn how to organize your thoughts. Write down a to-do list or set up calendar reminders so that you don't forget to complete certain tasks on time. Use a planner or notebook to organize your day, create outlines, and put your ideas in writing. Plan ahead and consider the kinds of hurdles that may come your way. The more prepared you are to take on your day, the more you will be able to minimize your stress. You'll also be better able to avoid stressful mistakes and rework.

Another way to minimize stress is to take a step back and look at your priorities and values. What matters to you? What things could you live without? Cut out the things you don't need to deal with. This may mean delegating some tasks to co-workers, family members, or roommates. Or it may mean removing something from your life entirely.

Remember: It's okay to say no to things. You don't have to take on every project that comes your way. If something is too much for you to handle right now, let it go so you can focus on what matters to you.

FACING STRESS HEAD-ON

At one point in my career, I was experiencing a challenging work relationship with a peer. I was becoming increasingly frustrated and stressed over the deteriorating relationship. During one face-to-face meeting, the peer addressed the situation directly.

She expressed her concern that we were not working effectively together. She was genuine and earnest. We talked through our different work styles and found a solid middle ground.

Within months, we were a great team and had eliminated the inefficiencies that had been consuming our time and fueling emotional angst. This was an amazing learning experience for me. I learned how to proactively address a stressful working relationship early and move forward in a positive way. **– Lynn**

A good goal is to address situations head on and get the issues resolved, but it's also okay to sometimes avoid stressful places, people, and tasks when they are prohibitive rather than productive. You'll still have to face some stressful situations, but not all of them. Look at what you can cut out altogether, and think about how you can minimize or better manage other sources of stress.

DEALING WITH STRESS

When stress does inevitably creep up on you, it's important that you know how to handle it. Whether you have to face it immediately or if it's a long-lasting bout that you can deal with privately, be prepared to address it efficiently and constructively.

If you're in a stressful situation in public or with another person (for example, a job interview or an argument), first remember to breathe. Inhale and hold for 5-10 seconds before you exhale. Slowing it down can help calm you immediately. You can also try to count to 10 before responding. Sometimes it is helpful to ask questions to clarify the situation. This gives you more time to understand and strategize the appropriate response. Reacting with negative emotions is usually not productive and gets in the way of problem solving. Instead of being reactionary, try to respond evenly. If you're at work, it may help to take a break. If you're having an issue with another person, you can ask to pick up the conversation a bit later after you've both had a chance to cool down.

PUTTING MY SKILLS TO WORK
A few years back I was overwhelmingly stressed at work, but I ironically felt lucky that it was happening after years

of acquiring the skills to work through it. The workload was intense, and on top of that, I simultaneously had several critical family issues. So how did I get through those four awful weeks?

1. Eliminating anything that was not urgent. For me, that meant spending less time on preparing dinner for the family—we ate a lot of a takeout and super simple meals.
2. Delegating and asking for help. There are always work and home tasks that you can hand off to your peers or family members.
3. Prioritizing what had to be done and when. A simple white board of critical projects, deadlines, and time-sensitive milestones within the projects did the trick.
4. Avoiding distractions. I turned my phone on silent and closed my email for blocks of time.
5. Playing my personal "calm" music playlists while I worked.
6. Taking a coffee break at Starbucks at mid-morning and an infused water break in the afternoon. Both were accompanied by a brief walk. This helped me refresh and enjoy some "me" time during the work day.
7. Enjoying a family break for dinner. I was able to hear about their days and enjoy their company.
8. Making sure I got enough sleep. While I needed to work extra hours, I made sure to get a decent amount of sleep every night. Reading a book for 30 minutes before bed helped me relax and stop thinking about work. – **Lynn**

When you have more time or privacy to deal with your stress, do something that you enjoy and that calms you. You may want to lie down for a moment to think or go for a run or get a massage. You can put on some relaxing music and just focus on the instruments. Remember to breathe. Allow yourself to clear your mind and process your situation, and try to find the bright side or a way you can face it. It can help to write something down or talk to someone, too. This will help you think clearly and get it off your chest.

It's important that you have a support group that you can turn to as well. Do you have friends, family members, or a loved one you speak with? Talk with someone, even if it's just for you to get the thoughts out there. You can ask them to just listen. If you want their advice or opinion, ask them what they think. Sometimes just talking can help, and you'll feel better knowing that you have allies on your side.

Try to find a way that you can deal with your stress, whether you prefer to do so on your own or with a close friend. Move through the stifling feelings of stress, and then prepare yourself to address the issue at hand.

MAKE TIME FOR YOURSELF

Dealing with stress is tough, and it can help to minimize stress in your everyday life. Make time for yourself each day. Even on days that are so busy the hours zoom by, give yourself at least a few minutes to relax.

Find calming activities that you enjoy or that bring you a sense of peace. Exercise and yoga are great ways to clear your head and improve your fitness. Meditation, reading, cooking, drawing, and playing music are all valuable ways to spend some free time and let your mind wander. Perhaps you want to go for a walk outside or get a manicure. Whatever you do, make sure it's something that you like and that allows you to free your mind a bit. Having hobbies is important in keeping you relaxed and happy, even on days that aren't stressful. They will be things you can turn to when stress is getting overwhelming and you need to recharge.

A MOMENT TO YOURSELF

I have an artist friend that starts her day every day meditating. She goes into a quiet place, and she sits with herself. I've never been able to master that, but I understand that it can be fulfilling and calming, and it can keep you laser-focused. I think that taking a walk, getting some fresh air, or just taking some time away—away from the computer, away from the hustle and bustle of everything that's going on—is really critical.

What I used to do every Sunday night was have a big bubble bath, and I'd have a glass of champagne or a hot cup of tea, and I would just soak, listen to music, and relax. That used to be my goodbye to the weekend and hello to the week ahead. I should get back into that habit. **– Tina**

You may want to make a serene space for yourself. You can set up a comfy chair, nice artwork, and even a little water feature to give you a serene place to go. Adding some of these elements to your workspace can also help make your job less stressful.

Remember to be mindful of your health. A healthy body and a healthy brain make stress far less challenging to cope with. Eat as healthily as you can within your budget, and find time to work out every week. Always allow yourself to get enough sleep—most people need 7 to 8 hours! In addition to the serenity practices we've outlined above, keep tabs on your mental and emotional self. If you notice that you are less able to cope with stress than usual, or if you have more burdens to carry, reach out to a mental health professional. There is no shame in getting help—only bravery.

EXPRESS YOUR STRESS

Sometimes stress will get the best of you—you can't avoid or even minimize everything. There will be stressful situations that you didn't see coming and can't get out of, or little stressful events will add up until you're ready to explode. Don't be afraid to express your stress. Bottling it up or holding it in is not healthy, and can ultimately cause health issues. Letting many stresses build up can lead to you overreacting to something later. Learn to let out your stress before it becomes overwhelming.

Some people express their stress by crying. It's okay to indulge in a good cry and let the tears fall. Maybe you let off steam by going for a run or banging on some drums. Listening to music can help others. Find a way to release your stress in a constructive manner.

You'll feel better once you've released some of your stress. You'll also feel more prepared to take on the rest of the day. There will always be some stress in your life, and as long as you're not bottling it up or pretending it doesn't exist, you'll be able to manage it.

At some point, most of us have an unfortunate and possibly inappropriate outburst. When it happens, do your best to stem the flow, briefly apologize, and disengage. You will need at least a few moments to collect yourself, away from the situation. First, remember that you're human, and emotions are normal and okay. How you respond after the outburst, when you're calm, depends entirely on the circumstances.

In some cases, your frustration was justified, and you might feel able to simply move on. In this case, you should still gauge how your outburst affected those around you and decide whether it should be discussed; you don't want to leave your peers disconcerted. Other times, your outburst might have been completely misplaced. You may even be written up. In these situations, apologies are certainly in order. Keep in mind, however, that sometimes apologies are not sufficient, and you may need to follow up with a change in behavior.

Oftentimes, your outburst won't be related to work at all, and is instead imported from outside stress. This will be true for the tantrums of others, as well. To avoid outbursts of your own and to deal with those of others, remember that you don't know what is happening in your colleagues' lives. Offer them the space they need, and be forgiving of their missteps, if possible.

Still, being on the receiving end of an emotional outburst can be challenging. Stay calm, and don't take it personally. Respond with respect and compassion. There are many different scenarios here; you might want to speak soothingly to the other person, or you might need to call for a supervisor. Make sure you are safe, and reach out for help as needed.

A LITTLE STRESS IS GOOD

Not all stress is bad! Throughout this chapter, we've talked about how to manage bad stress and not allow it to take over. Still, you can put some stress to good use, like motivation, reevaluation, and stamina.

Stress can help push you to accomplish your goals and do your best. It can also help you focus when a deadline is looming. How many people do you know who seem to work best as the deadline gets closer? Remember the college all-nighters to finish an important project or cram for an exam? Some of us need a little stress to perform.

If you avoid all stressful situations, you may not be allowing yourself to grow and learn. Some things in life will be scary at first, but once you face them, you will evolve. For some people, public speaking is so stressful that they will avoid it at all costs, but if you face your fears and give a presentation, you may find that it's not so bad after all. It will help you rise up to your challenges and advance in your career. If you feel that certain fears are holding you back, try to overcome them. You'll feel some stress—or maybe a lot of stress—but in the end you'll be proud of yourself.

Be cognizant of what kind of stress is good and how much is too much. Prolonged or chronic stress is both mentally and physically unhealthy and can become counterproductive. If stress is getting in the way of doing things well or is taking over your mind, you may need help with handling stress. Going to stress management classes, talking with a supportive friend, or seeing a therapist can help you to explore ways to reinterpret situations, activities and people in a way that is less stressful. Perhaps some activities can be reduced or rearranged, or you can organize your time differently. Maybe there are certain people or activities you need to avoid. Don't worry about a little stress in the day, but do be mindful if the stress is constant or overwhelming.

RECAP

Stress is a normal part of everyday life, and it's important that you know how to address it. How well do you manage your stress? Answer the following questions to see how you're doing and where you can use some improvement:

1. What are the sources of your stress? Do you put a lot of pressure on yourself? What kinds of stress are you prepared to encounter?
2. How do you minimize stress? Are there certain things you can cut out in order to limit your stress? Are there certain things you should avoid?
3. How do you deal with stress? Do you have a favorite method for facing it? When can you immediately address stress?
4. How do you spend your "you" time each day? What are your favorite hobbies? Do you give yourself time to relax every day?
5. Do you bottle up your stress? How do you release your stress?

6. Name a time when stress helped you push harder and achieve something important. Have you ever faced a fear and overcome the stress that once held you back?

PLAYLIST

We all know music is a great way to decompress during a difficult day. Our playlist provides inspiration to get you through: http://p2q.link/chapter6

CHAPTER 7
NETWORKING

YOU'VE PROBABLY HEARD the saying, "It's not what you know, it's who you know." While being knowledgeable in your career will always benefit you, knowing the right people can help you at work or during your job hunt. Based on the popular idea of there being only six degrees of separation between any two individuals, you are only ever seven people away from the person you need to know for a given situation.[1]

Whether this exact number is true or not, we know from experience that we live in a small world, and the people we meet today we are likely to run into again in unexpected places. Building a strong network of professional and personal connections is key to having a successful career.

SYMBIOTIC RELATIONSHIPS

Why, exactly, does "who you know" matter so much? Whether you're trying to land a job or about to close a deal, having the right connections will bring you and your work credibility. If you're in good favor with someone that your interviewer or potential client respect, they are more likely to trust you and the quality of your work.

THE CIRCLE OF NETWORKING
Early in my career, I was introduced to my colleague's husband. He was in the financial field and worked with a group of venture capitalists that were funding small, niche retailers. He asked me to come in and make a presentation regarding a customer acquisition program that I had developed. The venture capitalists really liked the program and began introducing me to their potential clients, suggesting that this was a program they might find very helpful to acquire new customers.

---

[1] Based on Frigyes Karinthy's short story, "Chains," in *Everything is Different* (1929).

> One of the clients I was introduced to actually ended up hiring my firm for this particular marketing program, and found it to be successful for them. That company's chief marketing person suggested to other agencies that they include my program in their overall strategy. One of the agencies she advised called me, which resulted in additional business.
>
> It's all about networking, and it's all about making sure that you're making your contact look good. So, I made my colleague look good because her husband was interested enough to introduce me to his colleagues, which, in turn, made her husband look good because his colleagues were interested, and then the colleagues looked good because the clients they introduced me to enjoyed the success of the program. – **Tina**

This is not to say that you should focus exclusively on connecting with the Top Dog kind of people who are well-known and well-respected. Make sure you make meaningful connections with your peers, as well. Keep in mind that the people just starting out may develop skills and expertise that will later be valuable to you. By keeping them in your network, you can help each other along the way for a mutually beneficial relationship.

KARMIC JUSTICE

> I knew a woman who began her career as the receptionist at a large company. In her role, she was treated by some people as if she was beneath them or insignificant—after all, she was "just" the receptionist and not of any importance.
>
> Eventually this woman worked her way up the corporate ladder and ended up in procurement. As you can imagine, the people who treated her poorly changed their tune immediately following her promotion. However, she never forgot who treated her with kindness and respect, and who treated her with arrogance and disdain, while she was the receptionist.
>
> When all criteria were equivalent, this woman awarded the business to people who had a positive relationship with her. No one wants to do business with

people who are disrespectful and have treated them badly in the past. Why would they? **– Lynn**

Keep in mind that everyone is worth knowing and connecting with, even those who are "below" you in the work hierarchy. Always be genuine and treat others with kindness and respect; never undervalue anyone, even the custodian—his life and his work is just as important as anyone's, and, without him, your organization wouldn't be able to run smoothly.

Everyone within your network has different insights and will have valuable input. If you find yourself in a jam, your network may be able to provide you with ideas of how to work out the problem. Different people's experiences and education will give them unique insights, so seek their advice. Their wealth of information will not only benefit you, but by asking for their input, you will make them feel appreciated.

As we've hinted at so far, most of all, networking is about helping people. By making these connections, you build a sense of community. You work together and help each other succeed by offering help when you can and connecting people who would benefit each other. They are symbiotic relationships that make sure everyone wins.

JUST KEEP TRYING

While you may recognize the importance of creating a network, that doesn't change the fact that it can seem *difficult*. It might help you to have a game plan. Use any previous knowledge you have to map out connections to get a sense of who knows whom and where their interests lie. A good starting point is to look at who is sponsoring the event you're attending or to look at the leadership team of a company or organization. You might gain a good idea of who might be a good starting point to introduce you to other people and what kind of topics they might be interested in discussing. As you meet people, make sure you write down where you met them on their business cards so you don't forget the context or the conversation, and then add those notes to their contact file when you enter the information to your computer or smart phone. This will help you in maintaining that connection.

If there's someone specific that you really want to meet, ask your network if they know them or know someone who knows them. People are generally happy to help, so don't be afraid to ask. Another way to meet a particular person or people in a particular field is to join organizations. Business and industry groups, as well as craft and art guilds, generally put on events or have meetings that will allow you to make valuable connections with people with similar interests or who have experience in skills that are useful to you.

An easy goal you can set for yourself is to meet at least one new person at every event you attend. Ask the people you know if there is anyone you should meet, or find the person who is standing apart from the crowd. Find common ground with everyone you meet—shared interests, both professional and personal, companies you've both worked at, or schools you've both attended. This will give your connection a personal touch and make it more likely to last.

Make sure that you are interested in what they are saying. People can tell when you are bored, and if you make them feel like you don't care about what they are saying, not only will that reflect poorly on you, but it will make them feel badly about themselves. Instead, listen to what they are saying and introduce them to other people in your network that you feel they should connect with. If you are talking to the person who was standing apart from the crowd, keep in mind that she may be shy or outside of her comfort zone. By maintaining interest in what she says and bringing her into your network, you will keep her comfortable and will earn her respect.

Perhaps *you* are the shy one who tends to stand apart from the group. If this resonates with you, networking may seem like a daunting task, and the goal of meeting one new person per event may seem impossible. We promise that it isn't. To follow the common adage, "fake it until you make it"—or in this case, pretend you're not shy. It may sound ridiculous, but playing make-believe that you are an outgoing person can work. Challenge yourself to talk to people in a way that you imagine a more extroverted you would.

THE FIRST STEP
Tina and I first met at a business dinner, which was a networking opportunity for peers at our company to meet one another. I wasn't sure I wanted to attend as I did not know any of the people well, and several of them (like Tina) I didn't know at all. While Tina and I did

not talk much at that dinner, we did discover that we shared a business philosophy. That was the beginning of a decades-long connection. All these years later, I am so grateful that I attended that networking dinner. It was the beginning of my amazing journey with Tina. **– Lynn**

Also, remember that everyone there is just like you. They are all trying to make connections, and they likely have similar experiences to your own in the workplace, in the classroom, or in life. If you are still struggling to come up with a conversation starter, it could help you to read the news. Open with a comment or a question about a recent news story—this gives you something to create human interest without starting with something that may seem too personal. Of course, be cautious about the news story you select. It might be unhelpful to begin with "Can you believe politician X? He is completely backward" only to find out that the person you're talking to is an enthusiastic supporter of politician X. Then again, this may help you choose your friends more wisely.

When it comes right down to it, though, the best way to learn how to network effectively is to try it. Practice makes perfect, and that adage holds true for striking up conversations and finding connections with people. You may fumble—we all do—but you will get more comfortable as you keep going, and the connections you make will introduce you to new people, and you will have that built-in common ground. If you feel out of place, the important thing is that you just keep trying. With each repetition, your confidence will grow, and soon you will master a new skill.

MAINTAINING YOUR COMMUNITY

It's not enough to just meet people, though. Remember, the point of building a network is to have people who will vouch for your character and work, as well as to build a community of people that help each other succeed.

Recall your goal to talk with at least one new person at each event you attend. Perhaps you will be ambitious and try to talk with as many new people as possible during the event. This is a great goal, but remember to give attention to the people you already know. Ask them how they are doing, what is new in their life, and if they have an opinion of who you should meet. This way you will strengthen your relationship with that person while also being directed to someone who can help grow your network.

Don't just wait to see them at conventions, though. Keep people engaged by emailing them about events or news that you think will interest them. Remember birthdays and work anniversaries. If you hear about them being promoted or switching to a new company, take the time to congratulate them. They will appreciate your thoughtfulness.

JUST A PHONE CALL AWAY
I like to stay in touch with people, and not just because I'm looking for business from them. Once I work with someone, they are stuck with me. I will put them on a rotation, and I will talk to them at least once a year—not looking for business, but just to be able to stay in touch and say, "Hey, how are you?" I think that people really appreciate it. I'll just pick up the phone and call, and if the phone number doesn't work, I'll do the same thing on LinkedIn. A phone call is a personal touch, though. It's just trying to find some form of commonality. That takes all of that awkwardness away for both of us during those conversations and keeps us close. I love getting updates from people because it's part of the fabric of our life. It sounds corny, but it's true! All those people that we meet along the way create who we are as individuals, and it's important to nurture those connections. **– Tina**

If you know someone who has a new job, new responsibility, or a new project, offer some help. Be ready to direct them to people and resources that can be useful to them. This will help build a community of giving and helping. Offer support to your network—not because you expect them to pay you back someday, but simply because you would be grateful for help in the same situation. Be compassionate in life and at work, not just for karma, but for the good of it.

CREATING LINKS ON SOCIAL MEDIA
Back in the days of snail mail and phone calls, keeping in touch was a little more difficult than it is today. Now we have social media like LinkedIn, Referral Key, and others, specifically for the purpose of maintaining your professional network.

LinkedIn can help you with many of the steps we have mentioned. It can show you connections between people before you even attend an event, so you know who to talk to and what their interests are, and it notifies you when one of your connections gets promoted or a new job. In this latter case, you have the perfect opportunity to show your support and provide insights into their new responsibilities.

As you meet people, connect with them on LinkedIn (or another service you choose) as soon as you're able. When sending the invitation, don't just stick with the generic message that LinkedIn provides you. Personalize it by reminding them where you met; say something like "It was great meeting you at the convention yesterday! I'd like to add you to my professional network on LinkedIn." That second sentence is what LinkedIn currently provides as the generic invitation. By adding that simple sentence before it, you are making a personal connection, reminding them of who you are, and letting them know that you put some thought into your invitation. LinkedIn also has Groups and Interests which allows you to connect with people that share your profession, your skills, and your interests.

Take advantage of social media to build and strengthen your network, and don't be shy about sending those invitations on LinkedIn. Connect with each person whose business card you collected, and keep in touch with them. Remember to be cognizant and respectful as to the nature of your relationship. This will help to build your symbiotic professional community.

"THEY WILL REMEMBER HOW YOU MADE THEM FEEL"

Poet, author, and civil rights activist Maya Angelou once said, "At the end of the day people won't remember what you said or did, they will remember how you made them feel." You can probably think of a few examples yourself of people who made you feel good and people who made you feel badly. Think of the impression you want to leave people with when you leave the room.

The first step is to make sure you are polite and considerate to everyone you meet, not just the CEO of your company. Receptionists, mail room technicians, and custodians are all worthy of your respect, so make sure you give respect and kindness freely. The warm feeling you leave them with should be worth this small effort, although you might also be paid back in kind—the receptionist may be more helpful in directing you to the person you need to see, for example.

A simple way to show your respect and genuine interest is to remember names. When someone introduces themselves, repeat their name back to them and collect their business card. If you are on the phone with someone, write down their name, and always be patient with them. If you have a hard time with remembering names, try to find some common ground with them. Robert Who Likes Musicals might be easier to remember than just Robert. Connect the face to the name and the name to an interesting fact about them.

EYES UP HERE
There is a gentleman that I worked for early in my career, whom I still see today at trade shows. He'll walk through the trade show, through the throngs of people, and only look at their nametags. If he sees a nametag that he recognizes, then he'll look up and say hi to the person. Or, if he sees a nametag of someone that he wants to meet, he'll look up because of the title that's on the nametag.

Other than that, the man will not look anyone in the face, which is so counter to what we're talking about: networking by being genuine and engaging. Some people may feel that networking is just a matter of getting as many business cards as you can, but what good is that? What do you do with them then? It's not a numbers game. It's a relationship foundation. By walking through the show and only saying hello to people who have the title or the company you're looking for, you're missing so much else about those individuals that may be helpful at some point in your career. You never know.
– Tina

When you remember their names, their jobs, and their interests, you can begin the conversation the next time you meet them with, "Hi, Robert! How's business? Did you watch the Tony Awards?" Robert will be flattered that you remembered his name and his love for musicals, and you will show that you were interested enough in what he was saying to commit it to memory.

As always, be kind and respectful. Try to keep your interactions with people on the positive side, keeping complaints to a minimum and focusing on shared interests and common goals. Make a conscious effort to leave people feeling good about themselves and about the interaction. Be an active listener, ask questions, and be complimentary if the occasion allows; the goal is to make a meaningful, memorable connection.

RECAP

Networking is extremely useful in your personal and professional life. While coming out of your shell can be difficult, the payoff is worth it when you build a mutually helpful community of professional connections. How good are you at networking? As you build this skill, ask yourself the following questions to keep yourself on track:

1. How do you value your network? Are you connecting with people from all levels, or only the Top Dogs? Do you seek your network's advice? Do you offer help to your network?
2. How do you approach networking? What is your game plan for attending events? What kind of goals do you set for yourself about how many people you will meet? Are you shy and in need of methods that work with or around that?
3. How do you maintain your network? Do you catch up with them at events? Do you keep up with their lives? How often do you help with their new endeavors?
4. What social media do you use to build your network? How do you personalize your LinkedIn invitations? Do you read the notifications of your networks' new jobs and promotions?
5. How do you make people feel when you talk to them? Are you respectful to everyone—even the custodian? Do you remember names and interests? What do you do to keep your interactions positive?

PLAYLIST

Get energized to make new connections with our playlist: http://p2c.link/chapter7

CHAPTER 8
FRIEND VS. BUSINESS RELATIONSHIP

"**Friendship is friendship;** business is business," or at least that's what Tina says. This may sound harsh, but it should alert you to the boundary between personal and professional life. We all want to make friends everywhere we go, and many of us seek to find those friends at work. Still, perhaps in business we should take a page from reality TV and repeat the mantra "I'm not here to make friends." When channeling your inner reality TV star, though, try to leave out the catfights and unnecessary drama.

CULTURE STUDIES

Before we get into things, we should point out that different companies have different cultures. Some places, especially start-ups and tech companies, tend to encourage open, friendly environments. They might focus on team-building and collaboration, open discussions between managers and employees, and staff may be frequently invited to after-work cocktails. On the other hand, some companies keep rigid hierarchies. These companies tend to be more formal, expecting a higher level of decorum than the carefree attitudes of those tech companies.

Whenever you're entering a new workplace, keep your eyes and ears open to the ways in which colleagues communicate. Pay attention to the company rules and policies. Observe the company culture and try to mirror it in your interactions with your peers and managers. This way you can avoid appearing too informal or too measured in your day-to-day dealings. In general, though, it's good to keep friendships and business relationships separate.

THE GREAT WALL OF PROFESSIONALISM

Making friends is exciting and fulfilling, but it is important to remember that business relationships are distinct from friendships. While friends are there to have your back, tell you what you need to hear, and take you on adventures, colleagues and clients have very different goals—i.e., business. It might seem obvious, but colleagues' and clients' main goals during your meetings are to benefit their employers.

Think of business relationships as having a wall of professionalism. That wall separates most of your personal information from the relationship. With business relationships, you can't get away with goofing around too much, and you have to maintain a certain level of respect.

Separating your personal and professional selves applies to how you interact on social media, along with maintaining privacy boundaries. Everything you put out there on any of your social channels becomes part of your personal brand. Be mindful of how others may perceive your posts and updates. It's a good policy to keep your personal and professional connections separate. With whom and how you connect through professional channels, like LinkedIn, is different than other social channels.

Embrace "think before you post" as an essential part of your social activities. While it may be important to you to share your passions, be aware of what you want to be public knowledge or publicly available. Ask yourself what you want co-workers, supervisors, executives, potential employers, or clients to know about yourself. This is especially true for respecting the privacy and confidences of others. You always want to be trustworthy, not perceived as overly intrusive or inquisitive.

An easy way to accomplish decorum that might *feel* unnatural without making it *look* unnatural is to make it about the person you're working with. Allow your colleagues and clients to share as much as they feel comfortable with, and reciprocate with some information of your own, like a pet's name. Especially with executives, let the other person lead the relationship so that you never come off as inappropriate.

THE STRUGGLE IS REAL

For some of us, not sharing too much will come easily. For others, nothing could be more difficult. Many people have trouble installing the correct filters to their mouths, but some would say that millennials have it the hardest. As a generation, millennials tend to be very open and honest, which in many cases is refreshing and endearing, but at other times can work against you.

At the risk of generalizing an entire generation, millennials, it is true, have grown up with social media, which encourages sharing—of everything. Microblogging and status updates keep our friends and followers up to date on our adventures and experiences, but the habit this risks creating is to always over-share.

ANTI-ANTIDEPRESSANT

At one of my previous jobs, I really struggled with keeping my personal life to myself. My colleagues were friendly and open, but I was unique in sharing all my personal details and life events. Growing up, I would tell my parents about my entire day in detail, and as a teenager I discovered Facebook and Tumblr. At some point, I developed a strong urge to tell everyone everything.

It got to the point where I would tell my boss about my ongoing battle with depression, the medications I was taking, and how many times each week I was seeing my therapist. I was lucky in that neither my boss nor my colleagues ever showed any malice toward me, but it did lead to some awkward situations. My boss tried to convince me that it was okay to take antidepressants for a short period, but that the goal should always be to stop needing them. I wanted to tell her that she obviously had no idea how depressions works, but for once I realized that sharing my thoughts might be a bad idea.

I'm lucky that the worst thing my over-sharing has led to is some unwanted advice. The people working at that office know far too much about my personal struggles. **– Rachel**

Learning to not over-share can be a real challenge if it's become a habit for you. Try to make a list of things that are off limits for business relationships—your love life, your relationship with your family, and your mental health might be on that list. Topics that you might want to avoid are ones that can either a) make the conversation awkward or b) be used against you by a manipulative individual.

KEEP POLITICS OUT

Writing during the 2016 US Presidential election, we *know* how difficult it can be to keep politics out of our conversations. For a lot of us, it's something that we're passionate about, and knowing someone's political alignment might be important to us. We joked in the last chapter that knowing someone's political leanings could help with choosing your friends more carefully, but remember that your business associates are not your friends.

If you're trying to work within your team or close a deal, it's safer to not offend the people you're with by voicing your convictions. With politics and social attitudes so closely bound, keeping your mouth shut about everything might feel pretty difficult because you want your colleagues to share your core values. To keep them separate, remember that your relationship with your colleagues and your clients is based on a product or a service. You can let your politics guide you to what companies you want to work with, but once you're in the relationship, it's best to keep politics off the agenda.

When a colleague or client begins talking about politics with you, as some inevitably will, stay quiet and listen. Try not to react to their opinions, whether they match yours or not. In the long run, people will admire your ability to stay apolitical and will respect you for your professional demeanor.

RECOUNTING AN ELECTION

For some reason, I am surrounded by people who are of a different political party than I, so I don't talk politics. The 2000 presidential election was very heated, as many people will recall, as to who actually won that election.

It happened that I was invited to the inauguration. I attended, and had really a fabulous time. But I didn't tell any of my clients or my colleagues where I was going until I came back. If anyone asked where I was, I said I was on the East Coast. If the follow-up questions were pointed enough, I would share the specifics about where I was.

It wasn't something I wanted to be outward about because it was such a divisive election. I didn't want to create problems where there didn't need to be any. My convictions are mine, and I don't feel that I need to put them on anyone else, whether they're a colleague or a client. At the end of the day, the people who found out I was there thought it was pretty cool, even if they didn't necessarily like who I had voted for. **– Tina**

MUDDLING THE WATERS

Of course, nothing in life is black and white, and this is true of business relationships. People like to work with people they like, and people like to be friends with people they like. Especially when you've worked with someone for a long time or if you're beginning work with someone you've been friends with for a while, the line between whether they're more of a friend or a colleague can get pretty blurry. This is okay, as long as you know how to navigate this multi-faceted relationship.

The rough part about this is that it can be difficult to go back and forth between being friends and being colleagues. You might try to switch between your "business hat" and your "friend hat," but you might find that your friend isn't comfortable doing professional work with you—and that's okay. When you're asking a friend to do business, make sure you put the question to them in a way that allows them an out, like "Are your comfortable doing this? I completely understand if you're not."

Another thing about friends is that you're allowed more slack with friendships. Being late, canceling plans last minute, and making jokes are things that are forgiven in most friendships, but they can be detrimental to a business relationship. Try to keep things professional when you're dealing with business—so be on time!

You also need to be professional when something goes wrong. When you work with someone, you can't rely on their friendship when you don't do your job correctly or if a project you did together went south. Don't expect them to cover for you—it's unfair to them as both a business partner and a friend. Instead, address the issue the same way you would with any other business relationship by being upfront about what happened, taking responsibility for your own mistakes, and finding a way to move forward.

When you're working with a client, the separation of friendship and business should be even stronger. Keep in mind that you both have a responsibility to your employers, so don't let your friendship force you into making a deal that isn't beneficial to your company. If your professional relationship gets too personal or informal, your superiors might see it as inappropriate. They might see you as possibly giving sensitive information to clients who shouldn't have it—so be careful.

> **LOCATION, LOCATION, LOCATION**
> I've always had an unwritten rule that friendship is friendship; business is business. There's definitely a line there between the two. One line has always been that I don't invite my clients to my house. I think that it just gets a bit personal when you see how the other person lives.
>
> For some reason, I became friendly with a particular client, and we started golfing together. On one particular instance, I invited this client to meet me at my house. It seemed the most logical place to meet if we were going to leave a car and drive together. Well, I have never heard the end of it. Because of where I lived, there were presumptions made as to what my lifestyle was and what my income might have been. I would never make that mistake again. **– Tina**

Getting too friendly with a business associate can be frustrating for you, too. Some people, whether they mean to be malicious or not, can bring up your personal information at inappropriate times or in unfunny jokes. Sharing personal information naturally takes place when you're friendly with a colleague or client, but keep it in check, especially if the person you're talking to makes you feel uncomfortable.

Remember, becoming friends with your co-workers is normal. If you are able to switch between Professional Mode and Friend Mode with relative ease, then such relationships might make your life more comfortable and your work more enjoyable. Just keep in mind what's appropriate when and where. However, if you struggle with these types of boundaries, you might try to keep the personal and professional spheres separate. Find what works for you.

BE NICE, BE HONEST

Overall, you want your demeanor to be positive toward the people you work with. Try to be happy, or at least neutral, when you're with colleagues and clients. But you don't necessarily have to fake it, either. If you're having a bad day, there is no shame in saying so—in fact, it will help you avoid misunderstandings. The goal is for your business peers to have a positive experience with you so that you can be as productive as possible during your meeting.

When it gets to the point of sharing information, you don't have to clam up. Instead, share news about upcoming projects you're working on, classes you're attending, or ideas you have for a new business. Some personal information is okay, too—people love to hear about pets and cooking adventures. Try to keep things light as you develop your professional relationship into one that is functional and friendly without being in each other's business.

> **EVERYTHING IN MODERATION**
> *There are times when it is important to share a vital piece of personal information. For the last several years, I have been coping with my husband's terminal illness. Rather than keep it to myself, I have let my co-workers, managers, and peers know that this is going on. I told them briefly and matter-of-factly. This was because I knew that I would have emergencies and ongoing challenges to schedule around. When I am asked how my husband is doing, I keep the answer brief and thank them for the inquiry. Then I get back to business.* **– Lynn**

Finally, don't be cold to anyone. Just because we're suggesting that you maintain a wall of professionalism doesn't mean we want you to shut people out and only engage with people you absolutely have to. Develop kind relationships with *everyone* you work with. Being kind and professional will lead to positive, respectful relationships that can last for years and years.

THE BUSINESS OF LOVE

We would be remiss to not address a major crossroads between business and personal relationships: love. It's natural to meet potential partners at work—you hear about couples meeting in the office all the time! After all, you spend a lot of your time at work, and the Office Romance is such a coveted trope on our favorite TV dramas.

But be smart. Be mindful of your behavior, and try to stay professional—your integrity and reputation are at risk. This isn't some *Scarlet Letter* warning, though. What we mean is that you never want to make your peers uncomfortable. Take the romance outside of the office.

In terms of client and vendor relationships, getting romantically involved is a very bad decision. It can become a major conflict of interest if the person you're trying to sell to is also your girlfriend or boyfriend—unfair discounts may be afoot! If you do enter a romantic relationship with a client, step away from that account. Give it to someone else who does not have romantic entanglements and will have clear judgment. This way you get to continue your romance without besmirching your and your company's reputation.

When you begin dating a peer, don't sneak around. Be upfront with your boss(es) and let them know that you and your colleague are together. It might be an awkward conversation, but the blowback of being caught after hiding the relationship will likely be much worse—your superiors may stop trusting you or your judgment. It sounds scary, but it is a possibility. Instead, just tell them. It's useful for them to know so they understand the dynamics of the office and how people might work together, so just keep it above board, and everyone will be happy.

RECAP

Knowing the difference between friendship and business relationships might seem unpleasant, but it can save you a world of hurt in the long run. How do you distinguish friends from colleagues? While you navigate professional relationships, ask yourself the following:

1. Are you aware of what the cultural norm is in your office? Are relationships formal or informal? How do people talk to their superiors?
2. How do you maintain your professional wall? What topics are off limits?
3. What do you do when a colleague or client brings up politics? How can you keep your cool while staying apolitical?
4. Why might your friendships and work relationships become muddled? How do you separate "friend time" from "business time"? Have you ever regretted sharing personal information?

5. Are you honest about your feelings with your colleagues? Do you maintain a positive attitude with your clients? Are you friendly with everyone you work with? What information do you share with peers?
6. Is an office romance worth the price? How can you avoid making work meetings uncomfortable with your lover? Do you notify your managers when you are dating a colleague? What could the effects be of dating a client or supplier?

PLAYLIST

Use our playlist to clear your mind and determine the best way to approach your professional relationships: http://p2q.link/chapter8

CHAPTER 9
DEALING WITH DIFFICULT PEOPLE

PERHAPS ONE OF the most frustrating truths in the world is the fact that you won't like everyone you deal with. Moms have told us that "people like people who are likeable," but some people just *aren't*. A lot of the time, you can avoid those people… but sometimes, you work with them 40 hours a week. How can you deal with these people without losing your mind? We're here to help!

CLASHING STYLES

Often, it's not that the person you're working with is mean or incompetent—it's just that their styles of working and communication are different from yours. If this is the case, then you can let out a "*whew!*" because that's an easy fix.

A good way to avoid conflict in this situation is to always have a clear agenda when you start a meeting. Make sure everyone knows what the agenda is before the meeting begins, and make sure all communications end with a clear takeaway—everyone should understand what they should be doing next, and everyone knows what was decided. The goal is to avoid confusion before, during, and after the meeting or call.

During the meeting, try to stay on task. You wrote out an agenda for a reason, so try not to let yourself get sidetracked. If there is something that comes up that should be addressed at length, schedule another meeting for that topic. On the other hand, you should be flexible. If someone brings up a concern or an idea, don't just shut them down because it's not on the agenda. Your agenda should have enough wiggle room for these discussions. But again, if it's going to take another hour to hash out, you should probably set up another meeting dedicated to that topic.

Your meetings and calls should all have goals—problems that need resolving, decisions that need making, updates that need giving, etc. Be clear and concise about what those goals are, and then pursue them without steamrolling over your peers. By following our agenda tips, you should be able to avoid some misunderstandings that could have started on your end.

Of course, you're not the only one in the conversation. You can work to make your own communication as crystal clear as possible, but that won't avoid every miscommunication. Try to recognize the unique working and communication styles of your peers. Are they team players, or do they prefer to work alone? Do they like to work with the details or the big picture? Are they bold in their statements, or do they tend to shy away from confrontation? Observe this, and then be prepared to discuss it.

If you and a peer are just not working well together, sit them down for a discussion of your working and communication styles. Be honest with what you prefer, and listen carefully to their preferences. Break down the walls that have built up by being understanding of their needs. Together, figure out what works best for each of you, and then find some common ground. If your peer needs things in writing, send emails rather than leaving voicemails. On the other hand, if you tend to read an aggressive voice in emails, have your peer call you instead so that you can hear the inflections in their voice.

People have different personalities and preferences. Recognizing, accepting, and finding the value in them will make your team stronger. By being flexible and finding common ground with your styles, you will allow everyone's skills to shine and your team will bring their best work. So be cognizant of your peers' needs, and you will have a better work experience.

CONSULTANT CONSULTATION
Over the years, all of us have worked or will have to work with people who seem difficult. I find this especially true now with so many virtual meetings. Several years back, a consultant was engaged on an initiative I was managing. We worked in different states, and all of our contact was by phone, email, or virtual meeting.

Our styles and thought processes were completely different, and I was struggling to find common ground, let alone build a good business relationship. I reached out to a colleague who knew both of us and asked for advice. The insight provided that the consultant and I wanted the same thing, but we were approaching the initiative from different perspectives.

After some quick review of the consultant's mindsets, I adjusted my language to better align our efforts. Everything started to fall into place, and our communication became far more effective. **– Lynn**

REVIVE YOUR ZOMBIE CO-WORKERS

Sometimes people just… don't do their work. They're zombies, shuffling along, doing the bare minimum, and never really contributing anything. They show few signs of life in terms of their work. If they're on your team or working on a project with you, they can bog you down and reflect poorly on you. In this case, it's not something as simple as a different working style—it's that they don't want to work.

If you have someone like this on your team, there are ways to motivate them, or at least get them to do what they need to. Returning to the agenda, make sure yours is very clear. Write down the tasks and the timeline for a project you're working on together. Once you do this, get their acknowledgment and consent on the agenda, tasks, and timeline—in writing, if possible. This eliminates their excuse of "no one ever told me" about their responsibilities, and it provides them the framework they may need to complete their work.

Try to create a positive atmosphere. We know that working with this kind of person is frustrating, but playing the "bad cop" will only create conflict. Your peer might feel bullied or resentful, and the conflict might be relayed to the superiors. Instead, encourage accountability by giving updates often, and then asking for updates in return. Let them know the work you've done this week, and ask them how their side is going. Be polite, but ask for details if they're withheld. Ask if they have any questions. This will open the door to a dialogue.

PULLING TEETH

I once had a customer service person that worked on my accounts from out of state. While he was very nice on the phone, he did not follow through with regularity. My clients would get in touch with me for answers and it became a very difficult situation.

> *We all have different working styles; as long as the goal is agreed to and achieved, the path should not matter. The only caveat here is that if someone is waiting on an answer, the courteous, professional action is to answer in a timely manner.*
>
> *It took quite a while to reach an agreement on our working relationship. This person needed a specific timeline and goal to be presented and managed for him. He was not a self-starter and was not able to think for himself. Clearly, he had the wrong position! Getting him to talk with me was like pulling teeth, but we eventually worked out our communications and he was presented with another career path—outside of customer service. It's easy to be happy when everything is going along well. The true challenge of the business relationship is how things are handled when things are not going as smoothly.* **– Tina**

If you have someone who is disinterested in their job, try to engage them with the work they're doing. Ask for their opinion on the project, and involve them in decisions. This will give them a feeling of ownership of the work they're doing. Provide more information about what the project is meant to achieve and why the work matters. People work harder if they feel proud of their work and valued by their peers. Provide these opportunities, and you can revive your zombie workers.

STAYING POSITIVE

Most of the people you work with will be pleasant, but some might be gloomy. Working with people who are predominantly negative in their outlook brings along its own set of challenges. They may well be hard-working with similar work styles and strong ethics, but they view almost everything from the "glass is half empty" perspective. They are often in a bad humor. It may seem like nothing can make them happy.

First, remember that you are not responsible for changing their dark view. Treat them with the same professional courtesy and respect that you do with everyone. Be proactive, and try for a more sober and serious tone when communicating with them. Don't change yourself, but be mindful that they will probably respond better when you speak in a more neutral manner. Also keep in mind that their "glass is half empty" outlook may illuminate a risk or threat to your project. It's important to find the balance between your different perspectives.

It's important not to allow someone else's negativity to invade your mindset. This is easier said than done, especially when you work side-by-side all day long. Spend your breaks and lunches apart. When leaving work, try shaking out all the negativity. Find what works for you.

As we recommended before, have a discussion with your co-worker about their attitude. Without being judgmental, let them know that, while you respect them, your different outlooks and personalities make you feel awkward at times. By talking with them, you may find middle ground so you can work more effectively together.

A good way to avoid developing bad relationships is to always be polite and cordial. Send thank you notes after meetings and introductions. Recognize that your colleagues are just people. Learn their interests and views. Find ways to make them look good to their superiors. They will appreciate your efforts, be kinder to you in return, and might even become more positive.

CONSTANT VIGILANCE

There are people with different work styles, there are zombies, and then there are people who are just downright mean. In your work, you might come across people who are dishonest and quick to throw their peers under the bus to preserve their own reputation. They have their own agenda, and they don't let anyone or anything get in their way.

When you're dealing with this kind of person, be attentive to your work and your communications with them. Don't let them trap you. Copy other people on your emails with them whenever it makes sense to do so, and include your peers on your calls if you can.

Get everything in writing. Don't rely on verbal communication with anyone, but especially not someone who is likely to try to undermine you. A good policy is to send an email immediately following a verbal discussion to clarify the conversation. But remember that email trails go both ways, so pay attention to the content, tone, and context of your emails. Maintain your professionalism with clear, concise, and respectful communication. It's a good policy to read your email carefully before sending. Save your emails for potential future reference. The goal when working with dishonest people is self-protection, so stay vigilant.

PULLING THE RECEIPTS

My experience with a new supervisor started innocuously. As usual, I was courteous, respectful, and reserved until her true character was revealed. The first thing I thought was a bit odd was that she wanted to have verbal discussions with only the two of us. During each call or meeting, I took detailed notes with the date and time of the meeting. Immediately following, I would send these notes in an email, CC'ing the appropriate team members. I also continued to provide weekly updates to our manager.

The first time the new supervisor attempted to throw me under the bus, I had backup because I had been following the best practices outlined. It was during a large, multi-department conference meeting, and it was the first time I had experienced a co-worker boldly lying in front of an entire group. After the momentary shock of the audience, one of my co-workers diplomatically corrected the supervisor's erroneous statement. I was very fortunate to have a few co-workers stand up for me.

After the incident, I doubled down, keeping meticulous notes and emails, avoiding one-on-one meetings and phone calls, and clearly communicating the content of those discussions to others when they could not be avoided. She continued to attempt to push me and everyone else under the bus, and working with her was unpleasant, but I learned a lot of skills from the experience. – **Lynn**

BAD BOSSES

One of the worst situations you can find yourself in is working for a supervisor with questionable ethics. They are willing to take shortcuts or commit fraud to make their department and themselves look good. You might find yourself being pressured to partake in ethically dubious, and possibly illegal, actions to keep your job, and that is a hard spot to be in.

Our best piece of advice is to get out ASAP. Try to find another position in another department or at another company. The longer you stick around, the more difficult it will be to avoid your supervisor's demands.

> ### GUILTY BY ASSOCIATION
> Once upon a time, I worked for a company that turned out to be practicing poor professional ethics. Obviously, I didn't know this prior to joining the organization. As time went on, the questionable company policies began to emerge.
>
> In my case, I recognized that even if I did not participate in the policies, I was putting myself in the position of being guilty by association. More importantly, I found the policies abhorrent, and that extended to anyone who went along with the policies, but especially to the leadership that had instigated them.
>
> My solution was to immediately initiate a job search. It took several months—I was careful not to take the first job offer just because I desperately wanted out. In the end, I left to a promoted position at a solid, reputable corporation. **– Lynn**

Of course, not everyone can just up and get a new job. If you can't get out, or if you can but you want to change things at your current job, contact Human Resources (HR). If you're asked to do something dishonest, don't. Go to HR, and tell them what your boss is telling you to do. Something that will help you in this situation is to have everything in writing.

As we said in the last section, copy other people on emails any time it makes sense to do so. In your follow-up emails, request that your supervisor confirm the takeaways, to clarify their meaning, and add anything that you did miss. Keep these emails. Document everything, and present it to HR.

The fallout might be unpleasant. Be prepared to stay calm and collected during the process, and always be professional. Instead of appearing vindictive, emphasize that the tasks you were being asked to carry out made you uncomfortable and that you worry about the reputation of the department and the company.

Having a dishonest supervisor can cause emotional stress. They might be cruel or their requirements might make you concerned about your own professional—and legal—future. Don't enable your supervisor to get to you.

Stay collected, remove yourself from the situation if you are able, and shut the whole thing down through HR—or even the Department of Labor. Maintaining your integrity is worth the emotional labor.

RECAP
Difficult people are an unfortunate reality in life and in work. They can bog you down or throw you under the bus for their mistakes. How can you deal with them without losing your mind or your job? Pause, count to 10, and ask yourself these questions when dealing with difficult people:

1. Does the bad relationship stem from different working or communication styles? How do they like to communicate? What are the values in their system? How can you find common ground?
2. Is your colleague a zombie along for the ride? Do they understand their responsibilities? How can you engage them in the decision-making process?
3. How can you stay upbeat when you work beside a pessimist? What can you do to communicate with them more effectively? When can you get away and focus on the positives?
4. Are you dealing with a dishonest co-worker? When can you copy your other co-workers on emails? How can you get every interaction in writing?
5. If your boss is dishonest, how can you get out of the situation? Can you find a new position within the company or at a new company? Do you have documentation to bring to HR?

PLAYLIST
Handling certain co-workers can be frustrating. Listen to our playlist and find the strength you'll need: http://p2q.link/chapter9

CHAPTER 10
BULLYING & HARASSMENT AT WORK

THERE ARE DIFFICULT people, and then there are *bullies*. They can cause you stress, they can make you cry in your office, and they can make you so miserable you can barely stand to come to work. Bullying and harassment at work are an unfortunate reality that many people face. What can you do to stand up to them? Sometimes the harassment is sexual—lewd pictures in your chat box or inappropriate comments when the harasser walks by. How do you shut that down?

WHY ARE THEY *LIKE* THIS?
During middle school anti-bullying assemblies, we were treated to explanations of why bullies behave like bullies, including low self-esteem and a troubled home-life. Unfortunately, you will find bullies well beyond middle and high school, and workplace bullies are every bit as nasty as schoolyard bullies. Let's try to explore why workplace bullies are so mean.

In a lot of ways, those middle school presentations were right. Bullying can be a defense mechanism to cope with feelings of low self-esteem or of being threatened. For bullies, being aggressive is a way to puff themselves up and feel larger and more important than they think themselves to be. If they think they are unappreciated at work, they may try to pull others down to try to stand out as an effective worker.

This might happen when the bully finds themselves in the wrong or if they've made a mistake. Their fear of being reprimanded or losing respect pushes them to assign the blame to somebody else. They pursue this end enthusiastically, throwing anyone they can under the bus so that their name remains untainted.

'CAUSE I'M HAPPY...
I had just become president of an organization, and there was a member that always showed me disrespect;

I would look out while conducting a meeting, and she'd be rolling her eyes or talking to somebody else, etc. She was very abrupt with me whenever we spoke. This went on for weeks.

I asked a couple people if I had done something wrong, but no one could figure it out. I finally asked her what I had done to offend her, and she said, "You're just so happy. It's disgusting. Nobody can be that happy." This woman took absolute offense to my being happy. In my opinion, it's a lot easier to be happy than it is to be grumpy, and I told her so. She eventually quit the club, but what a silly thing. I guess some people just have so much going on in their lives that they can't understand when people are perky. **– Tina**

Of course, there are a myriad of other reasons that people might be bullies—the above is just a common one. We can imagine that some people bully people just because they like getting the reaction, or maybe they just don't know any better. It can help to understand why a bully is behaving so horribly, but when it comes down to it, it doesn't really matter. Their behavior is inappropriate and must be put to an end.

BRAVING A BULLY

When someone is emotionally abusive to you, don't just suffer in silence. Talk to your supervisor or to HR until the problem gets resolved. Come prepared with documentation of the bullying, and bring in a witness if possible. Show that this person's behavior is a problem so someone with authority can rectify the situation.

This isn't about being a snitch. First of all, you deserve better than that. Everyone deserves to be treated with basic decency and respect, and you should not tolerate being treated poorly. Secondly, if they're doing it to you, they could also be doing it to other people. If the bully thinks they can get away with their wretched behavior, then they will continue with it, escalate it, and do it to more people. By bringing a bully to the attention of their supervisor and HR, you are doing the entire company a favor by nipping the behavior in the bud.

BEATING BACK BULLY

When I was in my early thirties, I was the recipient of

bullying by a departmental head. When I went to his department to check on the status of my projects, he would slam folders down on his desk and raise his voice. When I called, he raised his voice, was abrupt, and would often hang up on me. With an email inquiry, he either never responded or, on the rare occasion that he did, he wrote in all upper case and was terse.

One of my core responsibilities at work was to properly manage my projects and keep them on track. Every project went through this man's department, so I had to find a way to work with him, but nothing helped. I complained to my manager about his behavior repeatedly, but it never resulted in a lasting change.

As the situation continued to deteriorate, I considered filing a formal complaint with corporate HR. I was hesitant to do this, fearing personal repercussions, but one day a colleague witnessed one of the head's routines. This co-worker encouraged me to file a formal complaint, pledging to be a witness if needed.

I met with our HR administrator. She reassured me that not only did I need to file a formal complaint, but that there would be no reprisals or backlash on me. After making the formal complaint, the department head's bullying behavior stopped.

My only regret is not taking action months earlier. I should have gotten HR involved after my first complaint to my manager failed to cease the bullying. I never should have tolerated that man's intimidation and aggressive behavior. **– Lynn**

Bullying creates an atmosphere that is poisonous to efficient work. Your performance will suffer because of the stress. The harassment likely makes the people who witness the encounter uncomfortable and worried. Bullying can be covert or overt. The negative effects are not limited to the targeted individuals, and may lead to a decline in employee morale and a change in organizational culture. These are all reasons why the supervisor and HR should be seriously concerned with bullying behavior.

But sometimes the company will do too little or nothing at all. Their talks with the bully might not lead to real or lasting change, and it might eventually get swept under the rug.

Indeed, bullying might even be occurring at the upper level of the company and is thereby enshrined as a company norm. If this is the case, it is a toxic corporation, and you need to get out if you can. Things are unlikely to change there without a massive push.

In the short term, if you are dealing with a bully, try to remember to be proactive rather than reactive. During the bullying, step away from the situation, even if you have to come up with an excuse like needing to make a phone call. Use that time to take a deep breath and gather your thoughts. Find a way to keep your head held high, and see if you can de-escalate the situation. Otherwise, find a way to ride it out until the bully finally walks away.

WORDS OF CAUTION

Before we move forward with this chapter, we want to provide you with two warnings: Be mindful of HR, and know the legality of your situation. You should always do what is necessary to end harassment, and understanding the possible obstacles will better prepare you for the fight.

Human Resources (HR) is typically who you should notify in cases of bullying and harassment. The employees there are usually sympathetic and understand the gravity of bullying behavior. Keep in mind, however, that HR is there to protect the company's interests. Generally speaking, stopping and preventing harassment *is* in the company's best interest, but be cognizant of the position of the person you're accusing. What kind of power and influence does HR have compared to the perpetrator? Are there actual policies and protocols in place to take care of harassment, or does the HR department provide empty promises?

Be thoughtful of what you are bringing to HR's attention, too. If you're just angry with someone for a one-off argument, you should avoid HR; there can be real consequences for being perceived as a troublemaker. When you do bring up bullying or harassment, provide evidence to support your claim. If the bully's behavior is of the illegal variety, most HR departments are required to and will document the claims and help you with legal counsel.

So, how do you know if your harasser's actions are illegal? The U.S. Equal Employment Opportunity Commission (EEOC) defines illegal harassment as violating Title VII of the Civil

Rights Act of 1964, the Age Discrimination in Employment Act of 1967, and/or the Americans with Disabilities Act of 1990. This means that the harassment needs to be "based on race, color, religion, sex (including pregnancy), national origin, age (40 or older), disability or genetic information" for the EEOC to be able to do anything about it. Harassment is illegal when it "1) enduring the offensive conduct becomes a condition of continued employment, or 2) the conduct is severe or pervasive enough to create a work environment that a reasonable person would consider intimidating, hostile, or abusive." Annoying co-workers might not rise to the level of behaving unlawfully.[1]

Again, you should do everything within your power to take care of yourself. Even if the behavior doesn't meet the EEOC's requirements to be considered illegal, if it's making you uncomfortable, try to fix it. You can try speaking to the offender directly, if you think that might help. Otherwise, you can ask the advice of co-workers, or talk to your supervisor about it. Do whatever makes sense within the context of your experience and your company.

CREEPY CO-WORKERS

This is a book by women, for women. Something that must be addressed is sexual harassment. We're no longer in the *Mad Men* days, but a 2015 *Cosmopolitan* survey found that one third of the over 2200 working millennial women surveyed had been sexually harassed at work. Another 16% said they had not been sexually harassed but had experienced sexually explicit or sexist remarks.[2]

CREEPY, CRAWLY

Early in my career, I worked with a department head who would constantly touch my arm, shoulder, or the scarf I was wearing. He never said anything inappropriate, although he often went overboard on the compliments. For me, it was creepy with a high "ick" factor. It just made me uncomfortable. I avoided him whenever possible. When I did need to talk with him in person, I positioned myself behind the work tables, keeping a physical barrier between us.

---

1 https://www.eeoc.gov/laws/types/harassment.cfm
2 http://www.huffingtonpost.com/2015/02/19/1-in-3-women-sexually-harassed-work-cosmopolitan_n_6713814.html

> *Looking back, the simple solution would have been to kindly tell him that I had personal space boundaries, and he was unknowingly crossing those boundaries. It was about me, not him, and I needed his help to maintain my personal space.* – **Lynn**

In Lynn's case, the harasser likely wasn't aware of what he was doing wrong. If this happens, be clear about your boundaries. Whether it's personal space or personal conversation topics, be direct about your preferences and needs. If they didn't mean to be inappropriate, they will have the opportunity to modify their behavior.

Some women can find it difficult to identify and call out sexual harassment. If you're unsure of what just happened, or if you want to draw attention to the situation, a good place to start is by asking the person to clarify what they just said or did. Ask them, "What did you mean by that? This is how I interpreted it." This gives the person a chance to reflect and explain, but it also gives you a moment to breathe and consider how you will respond to the situation.

Oftentimes, the most common forms of sexual harassment are subtle. Someone may make inappropriate comments and jokes, and then claim that you are "too sensitive" when you get offended. Remember that this boorish behavior *is* harassment because the intent is to belittle and denigrate. Tell the person that what they've said or done is unacceptable. If they persist, and if you feel safe doing so, ask if you can film them on your smart phone to let HR decide. Use today's tools to protect yourself from egregious conduct.

If the harassment is malicious, do what you can to minimize your contact with them. Avoid being alone with your harasser, and notify a supervisor of what is happening. If getting your supervisor involved is not enough to deter the harassment, talk to HR. As with bullies, if this person is harassing you, they are likely to be harassing others, as well.

Sexual harassment is never excusable. If notifying HR does not resolve the issue, the company will have shown itself to be indifferent to sexual harassment. In some cases, you will have the evidence and persistence to take a case to the EEOC. Bureaucracy can be slower than molasses in January, and the case may take years to settle, but you will have made it clear to the company that sexual harassment is not okay.

CONTROL YOUR TEMPER

As you need to watch out for bullies, you also need to keep an eye on your own behavior to make sure you yourself are not becoming a bully. Don't be a shrinking violet, but make sure you aren't being overly aggressive with your co-workers, either. Be polite and respectful at all times.

Receiving criticism can be difficult, but if you are told that you make someone uncomfortable, listen. Understand their concerns, and then think about how you can adjust your behavior to be more respectful. Apologize when you treat someone poorly, and make sure you avoid that treatment in the future. Everyone slips up every now and again, so don't be too hard on yourself, but be more mindful in the future.

Sometimes a bad day will cause you to lash out. You might yell at a co-worker or display some physical aggression that intimidates your peers. While many of your co-workers might be able to sympathize with whatever plight you're facing, tantrums are never acceptable—they often make the people around you feel nervous, uncomfortable, or even angry. Just take to heart what you learned as a child: control your temper.

LOSING CONTROL

I had an assistant, Jill, who was just the calmest person. Early in my career, I rode an emotional rollercoaster—I was always up and down. I would get anxious and a little bit hyper.

One day, I had come in, and there was just so much that had piled up. There was some business that I thought was coming in that I found out wasn't, and it was too late in the day to reach anyone back east. I was so frustrated, I walked into my office, and I took my car keys, and I threw them across the room. They hit the wall, and I shocked myself that I had done it.

Jill came in and took everything off of my desk, everything within reach, without saying a word, and then she left and shut the door. She taught me a life lesson that day: There is never anything that is that important in business. Unless you're doing brain surgery, there really isn't. There is nothing to lose control over. **– Tina**

As is so often the case, it comes down to treating others in a way that you would want to be treated. When you are talking to someone, consider how your words might sound to them and how they might make them feel. Of course, sometimes you need to express criticism, but make sure you do it in a way that doesn't demean them as a person. Be flexible with your peers, and don't sweat the small stuff. They will appreciate your patience.

BE MAGNIFICENT

A positive environment is a more successful environment, for you and the entire team. You can't control others' behavior, but you can be cautious about getting into bad situations. Avoid bullies, but be respectful to everyone—including the bullies.

To discourage bullies from targeting you, and to keep yourself from becoming a bully, remember to do the following: Present yourself as powerful and confident. Remember that you are a competent professional who deserves respect and knows how to be respectful to others. People will be impressed by your professionalism and the power you exude. *Be magnificent.*

When you are facing a bully, don't let them drag you down to their level. It is natural to want to strike back, but try to be the bigger person. Show everyone that you are stronger and more mature than your bully. And keep in mind that there is a lot of power in just walking away—you don't have to engage your bully in a screaming match. Demonstrate that you will not waste your time being treated with disrespect.

THIS CONVERSATION IS OVER

At one time, a company I was employed with did a lot of work with another company that had an explosive chief executive. This person's reputation of having a short fuse was well known within the industry, but we continued to work with this company because they did excellent work and otherwise had a pleasant, helpful staff.

One day, I received a call from the volatile chief executive regarding a project. Within a few minutes, this person was shouting profanities. I firmly interrupted his tirade and told him that I would not continue the conversation if he did not stop yelling and swearing. He reacted with more shouting and profanities, so I responded by hanging up the phone. I refused to accept his call minutes later.

> I went to my manager's office to notify him of what had occurred. While we were discussing it, the chief executive called my manager. My manager asked me to wait while he took the call. Sure enough, the executive started shouting that I had hung up on him. My boss said that if the executive did not calm down and moderate his tone, he would do the same thing. The executive continued to yell, and my boss hung up.
>
> The next day, my boss went to see the executive at his office. He notified him that our company would not be able to continue to work with his company if the executive did not treat our employees with professional respect. From then on, when our employees had to work with that executive, he maintained self-control. **– Lynn**

On the other hand, if you witness someone else being bullied, *do something*. Stand by your colleague throughout the abuse, directing your attention to them and not the bully. Once the bully leaves, reassure your peer that they do not deserve such treatment, and provide them some comfort. Give them the opportunity to report the abuse themselves, but offer to do it for them if they would prefer it. Be willing to corroborate their complaints to their supervisor and to HR. Let them know that they have someone on their side.

RECAP

Dealing with bullies and harassers is one of the most uncomfortable things you might have do in your work life. When tackling this challenge, ask yourself the following questions to keep yourself on track:

1. Why does the bully behave this way? Are they feeling threatened at work?
2. Can you demonstrate the bullying to HR? How is the behavior affecting the team? Is bullying a cultural norm at your company?
3. In cases of sexual harassment, does the harasser realize their inappropriate behavior? How can you avoid your harasser? Do you need to take your complaints even beyond HR?
4. Are you aggressive with your co-workers? Have you been told that you intimidate people? How can you control your temper?

5. How can you exude power and confidence? Are you able to walk away from a bully? How can you help a colleague who is being bullied?

PLAYLIST

Music can give you the peace of mind necessary to face your adversaries and nurture your support network. We have just the playlist for you! http://p2q.link/chapter10

CHAPTER 11
MENTORS & SUPPORT STRUCTURES

When facing the challenges that will crop up throughout your career, remember that you don't have to weather the storm alone. Finding people to help guide you is incredibly valuable as you start your career or enter a new job. Mentors share their experience and advice to help you grow as an employee. Having someone who wants you to succeed and can show you how to do that will be a great comfort to you.

But you also need support outside of the workplace. Building a support network of your friends and family, as well as contacts from outside organizations, is vital to maintaining your sanity as you navigate your career. They provide outside perspectives on your challenges, and they give you a chance to express yourself outside of your job.

A HELPING HAND

Entering a new job can be intimidating. You might feel out of place, even if you know how to do your work. As a new employee, it's good to become a part of the office culture. Engage in your co-workers' conversations so you can get a feel for the vibe of the workplace and gauge what the attitudes in your field are.

This is more difficult than it might sound, but it's easier if you have a mentor. Some young people have been coached throughout their lives by family and friends on how to be a successful employee in your field. Others, however, have not. People new to the workforce sometimes make the mistake of thinking that they have to find their own way without any help. Not true! We all need help, so make a point of going out and finding it.

A mentor is someone who's been in the field or at that company longer than you have and can show you the proverbial ropes in both the work you're doing and the company culture. They are someone who can discuss with you the challenges you're facing, and the two of you can talk through them.

Sometimes all you need is someone to let you talk and listen with empathy. You can work out a lot on your own if you have someone to bounce ideas off of. Other times, you might need some advice from someone who has faced the challenges you are facing. In this case, letting your mentor talk and listening closely can be very helpful. They will impart the lessons they learned so that you can learn from their experiences.

WOOING A MENTOR

So, it's settled: You should find a mentor—but how? In rare instances, someone might float down from the clouds and offer to be your mentor, but in the real world you will typically need to seek out a mentor yourself.

ALL YOU HAVE TO DO IS ASK

I'd gone to work for a new company, and during the training/onboarding process, there was a gentleman that I found myself continually going to for help. I thought we had a very good rapport.

There was so much to learn and so much to know, and this fellow had been with the company for decades. So, I asked him if he would mind being my mentor. He was really taken aback by my direct question, but he agreed to be my mentor.

Sometimes mentorship doesn't just happen—sometimes we have to go out and ask. **– Tina**

Perhaps you will approach someone and ask directly for them to be your mentor. This is a straightforward approach, but one that many might find unnatural. More often, finding a mentor will come more organically, and you might not even think of your mentor as being such—they might just be a friend in your mind. Still, they are a calming presence for you and offer sound advice, and that's what mentoring is all about.

No one likes to be labeled a "brown-noser," but the reality is that there are always opportunities for genuine compliments. When you're starting out a new job, go out and meet the people around your office. Find someone who has a similar working style to yours or someone who you are drawn to, and ask to have coffee with them, even if they're at a managerial level or in another department. People will be delighted to hear you say, "I'm new here. You seem like you've got a handle on things, and I would appreciate your advice." During your conversations with your intended mentor, be engaged and curious. Ask them how long they've worked there and how they got the position. They will appreciate your interest!

The goal is typically to be able to do some projects with your mentor to watch how they manage their tasks and teams, but even just occasionally meeting your mentor for coffee or lunch is helpful. Having someone who wants to see you succeed will give you a lot of confidence and provide a great foundation for your career.

If you're having a hard time finding a mentor at your company, don't worry! There are a lot of organizations out there that you can join where you will find people who can help you. The National Organization of Women Business Owners and local groups like the Women's Business Exchange in Seattle are just two examples of organizations full of people who want to help each other succeed. Check to see if there are any professional or trade organizations in your field. While you're building your network (see *Chapter 7*), seek your contacts' advice. They might be able to become your mentor or put you in contact with someone in your field who can help you. Alternatively, there are also formalized professional mentoring programs that you can join, or you can seek a professional guidance counselor if you are going through something difficult.

When you're starting a new job, try to have a few colleagues in your corner ASAP. During the interviewing process for the position, ask the interviewer, "What makes someone successful here?" and, "What is the company culture here?" These questions are great to pull out during an interview—you will appear engaged and forward-thinking—but they will also set you on the right track to find a mentor quickly once you get hired. Having a few people who you can touch base and talk with early on will alleviate your stress and make you feel more comfortable.

OUTSIDE PERSPECTIVES

While having a mentor at work is helpful, having a support

system outside of work is vital. You need to be able to talk about work with people who are outside of it, and you need to be able to remove yourself from your job to relate to peers on other planes. Ask for advice to gain new insights on situations you are encountering at work. The ability to see an issue from a new perspective is invaluable and can foster a creative solution. In turn, give your thoughts openly when asked, or offer when you see a peer frustrated. It frees you to be a whole person, and you know that you'll have friends to depend on if you leave your job.

Finding your support network can happen in many ways, and you'll find friends from a variety of contexts. If you're still looking for a support network or if you've moved to a new city, you have a lot of options. Join a group that matches your interests—a book club, volunteer organization, or a *Dungeons & Dragons* guild. You can use websites like MeetUp.com to find the perfect club for you. These are people with whom you will share a common interest and have something to relate to, and you can build your relationship from there.

WOVEN TOGETHER
You can find mentors in unexpected places—I did when I joined my local knitting guild. When we would meet monthly, we talked, shared stories, and had a sounding board for challenges. While none of these women were in my industry, they had a wealth of experience and hard-earned knowledge. They were generous with their wisdom and provided great encouragement.

Every meeting was relaxing, healing my stress of the day. I learned a great deal about knitting techniques, but even more about life and work by being surrounded by a supportive group of women. **– Lynn**

You don't have to draw your entire support network from the same place. Build a broad support network that feeds your soul on many different levels and provides different types of comfort and communication. Your activist friends, the friends you play video games with, and the friends you have deep, personal conversations with offer varying types of support, and they are all important. They speak to different parts of your personality, and your whole you deserves to be recognized and expressed.

Having a support network outside of work is so important. They are an outlet from the stress of your job, and they are catalysts for different sides of you. Moreover, these friends will have their own experience and advice to share with you that differs greatly from the mentors within your field. All perspectives are important, and the ones your support network provide are influenced by their varying life journeys.

PAYING IT FORWARD

Mentors gain from the mentoring relationship, too. The opportunity to teach or advise others can increase the mentor's confidence and their own job satisfaction. The mentor is required to listen to the concerns of the employee and may develop a better understanding of employee issues and learn stronger communication skills. If the mentor is a supervisor, mentoring can improve her supervisory skills. Even if a mentored employee leaves the company, the mentor and mentee may maintain a professional connection. This may expand the mentor's reputation and connections.

Whether the art of mentorship is truly endangered or not, as some claim, it's definitely something worth learning. The point of a professional network is to become a community that helps each other out. One great way of doing that is relating to others your experience and your advice—i.e., being a mentor. It also helps you build up your own reputation as being someone who is reliable and knows how to do her job.

KEEP AN OPEN DOOR

My first mentor was a seasoned and successful professional who was assigned to have me tag along and observe how he did his job. It was informal job training, but I learned more from my two weeks of observation and conversation with this person than I would have in a more formal mentorship.

With such a great experience and example, it established my foundation of helping people get started and find their way. It's important for all of us to not just encourage the new team member, but to be selfless in showing them how to be successful. Every organization and industry has unique inside knowledge, and sharing that knowledge goes a long way in helping someone find their balance.

> Keeping an open door to questions and the general puzzlement of why something is done in a particular way rewards everyone. Not only is it supportive and welcoming to the newcomer, the newcomer brings a fresh perspective. It's amazing how positive that can be to shaking up the paradigm.
>
> Take the exciting opportunity to help your co-workers whenever you can. Even if you've only been at the company a week, sharing which lunch room microwave is glitchy will be useful for the new member. Every little bit adds up. **– Lynn**

Learning to be a mentor is just like any new skill: It's about acquiring base knowledge and repetition. You may think that you have nothing to offer, but that's not true. Even if you've only been with the company for a month, you'll still have acquired some inside information that would benefit someone on their first day. It might be a shortcut to the conference room, the easiest way to file reports, or the scoop on the closest coffee stand. While being helpful does not in itself qualify as mentoring, it will start you on the path to learning to become a mentor.

You can begin a mentoring relationship casually. If there is a new employee that you see has a lot of potential, go introduce yourself. Ask how they are getting along at the company and what they're working on. Invite them to lunch. If you see someone struggling, ask what is going on, and see if you can help. Be available for others to come to you for help. And remember, forcing a mentoring relationship on someone may not be well-received, so ensure that your intended mentee actually wants some guidance.

If you are fortunate enough to work for a corporation or belong to a professional organization that has a formal mentoring program, take advantage and participate. You will learn a lot about mentoring and be able to apply that knowledge to become a mentor yourself. Even without a formal program, you will learn how to mentor by being mentored yourself. Strong leaders know that no matter how far in the industry they rise, they need a mentor to continue their growth. Once you've reached a level of expertise, you are in a position to help others by mentoring them, even while you continue to be mentored yourself.

RECAP
Finding people to be in your corner can be tough, but getting a mentor and building a support network are important to navigating your career. Knowing that there are friends and colleagues who want to see you succeed will make you more confident, so when you're searching for these people, ask yourself the following questions:
1. Do you engage with your colleagues at your new job? Why do you need a mentor?
2. Who do you admire in your workplace or in your field? How can you block out some time for the two of you to have a conversation? What other organizations are available to you that might help you find a mentor?
3. Who can you turn to outside of your office? What groups are there that interest you where you might find friends? Do you have an outlet from your work stress?
4. How can you become a mentor? Is there someone at your workplace that you see potential in? What experiences and advice can you impart to others?

PLAYLIST
Finding a mentor or becoming one yourself is easier with the perfect playlist: http://p2q.link/chapter11

CHAPTER 12
BREAKING DOUBLE STANDARDS

EQUALITY IS A process, and the progress women have made during the last century has been immense. Still, you might find yourself facing some double standards at the office that might leave you feeling like you woke up in the 1950s. If you're lucky, you won't ever experience it, but gender bias is still very real for many young women entering the workforce. We're still talking about breaking glass ceilings, after all, and, with that, we should be shattering double standards.

SPEAKING UP

The Geena Davis Institute on Gender in Media found that when a movie shows a crowd of people, just 17% of them will be women.[1] Davis explained in an interview with NPR that this is because "if there's 17 percent women, the men in the group think it's 50-50. And if there's 33 percent women, the men perceive that as there being more women in the room than men."[2] PBS reports that in mixed company, men tend to talk more than women, but if women are encouraged to speak 50% of the time, they are perceived as receiving more than their "fair share" of speaking time.[3]

Unsurprisingly, this is often true in the workplace, as well. Women who talk the same amount as men, or even slightly less than men, during meetings or presentations are seen as taking over the discussion. People expect men to talk more, but they don't usually realize that this is the case. Moreover, when women do speak, they are a third more likely to be interrupted than men.[4]

---

1 http://seejane.org/wp-content/uploads/GDIGM_Gender_Stereotypes.pdf
2 http://www.npr.org/templates/transcript/transcript.php?storyId=197390707
3 http://www.pbs.org/speak/speech/prejudice/women/
4 http://www.forbes.com/sites/womensmedia/2017/01/03/gal-interrupted-why-men-interrupt-women-and-how-to-avert-this-in-the-workplace/#67b0e1ee5fba

What's worse is that men are often given more credibility than women. A woman may give facts and figures or give good advice, but men (and even women) often won't hear it or won't listen. A woman will have to repeat herself again and again before she is acknowledged, but if a man says the exact same thing, he has immediate credibility. How many times have you made a good point or even a good joke and have it ignored only for a man to repeat what you said and receive all the accolades? It's maddening!

IT NEVER HURTS TO ASK
When I was invited to speak at a customer's conference, our CEO not only decided to attend, but wanted to speak during a portion of my presentation. This was an interesting situation for me. Our CEO had always treated me, and all the other employees, with respect. However, I was curious as to why he felt the need to attend and speak during my presentation.

Rather than feeling threatened or somehow lacking, I asked him why he wanted to attend and speak at the event. His response was that he wanted to be there to demonstrate the company's support of me and our commitment to the client. When something like this happens, it's important to speak up and ask questions. Remember not to make assumptions—the actual motivations may surprise you. – **Lynn**

So what can you do? There is no easy fix, but a good start is to look people in the eye when you're talking to them in person. Make sure you have their attention—if they're looking directly at you, it's reasonable to expect that they're listening. If you're speaking in a group, choose someone, like the department head or manager, to address, and then look into their eyes. You might have to draw their attention to be able to make eye contact, but it's worth raising your voice and saying, "John/Jane, you'll appreciate this..." just so you know that they're paying attention.

In a virtual meeting—or in any meeting—make your statement, and then be quiet and wait for a response. People, especially women, have a hard time with dead air, but it's important to allow people to gather their thoughts and formulate a response. It also makes your words more powerful if you allow your statement to stand alone rather than continue to talk just to fill in the silence. Allow your peers to absorb what you said.

In the same vein, don't instantly respond, either. When others are speaking, take a moment to process what they are saying before you jump in with your answer. Always make sure that you develop an articulate and intelligent response so that your thoughts are delivered most effectively. Not only will you look smarter, but you will be able to express more of your thoughts and opinions before men start thinking that you're talking too much (wink, wink).

On the other hand, be present. If you have something to say, *say it*. Speak up so that you give yourself the opportunity to make your thoughts known. Always remember that you deserve to be at that table and that you deserve to have a voice, not just to facilitate the conversation, but to add to it and even change its direction. This is your company, too, so don't let the men talk over you.

> **MAKING SURE YOU'RE HEARD**
> *Throughout my career, I've attended many seminars, sales meetings, and the like, and there's always time for asking questions and giving comments. For much of my career, I was a person that would just sit back and listen. I still do, but I've noticed that men have a tendency to always speak up. They may not have anything to say, but they feel like they need to be heard so somebody remembers them.*
>
> *I think that's a place where women as a whole can do a better job, in being heard. I can't imagine making a comment that makes absolutely no sense to the topic, but that's what men seem to do, and they're remembered because they spoke up. Now I continue listen, but I also make it a point to always have something to say in a meeting, even if it's just asking for clarification.* **– Tina**

FAMILY MATTERS

It is a truth universally acknowledged that a woman of reproductive age must be in want of children—if they don't already have some. This statement is just as ludicrous as Jane Austen's first line of *Pride and Prejudice*, but it's believed, consciously or not, by a lot of people. You will find some of these people in business.

SHOULD I PUT A RING ON IT?
When my sister was in her mid-20s, she was newly married and looking for a job. She and her husband had agreed that they wouldn't have children for at least four years after their marriage—if ever—but my sister was afraid of the assumptions that interviewers might have if they saw her wearing a wedding ring. The question of whether to wear the ring burdened her throughout the job hunt because she didn't want to be dishonest, but she also didn't want hiring personnel to be nervous about hiring a woman they feared would soon take maternity leave.

Ultimately, my sister decided to wear her wedding ring for interviews (although she awkwardly tried to keep her left hand out of view), but this is a question that shouldn't even occur to women—and certainly doesn't occur to men. My sister did get a job in her field, and she is living happily with her husband and their cat with children still far from her mind. Would she have gotten a job faster or a better position if she hadn't worn her wedding ring? We'll never know. **– Rachel**

While making assumptions about a woman's reproductive future is never okay, a lot of women *do* have children. This comes with its own set of inequalities and double standards. Women are often perceived as constantly taking time off to take care of their children, and this is viewed as an inconvenience to the company. Women face a double-edged sword of both being expected to take time off for children (as opposed to the children's father) and being reprimanded for taking time off. Meanwhile, when men take time off for their children, they are hailed as being great dads.

In this last case, if you notice inequality in the treatment of men and women taking time off work for kids, call it out! If your boss is giving you grief for wanting to leave early to attend your daughter's karate competition, point out that they let your male coworker leave early to go to his son's baseball game last week. Sometimes your manager won't realize the bias in their treatment until you bring it to their attention.

Of course, if you're without children, you might be left wondering why your parent co-workers are afforded time off for their children while you are kept in the workplace. Non-parents have responsibilities, too! As we said, it is ludicrous to assume that women automatically and invariably desire children—many women don't. Sometimes, these women are called selfish or are told that they will change their minds, as if co-workers would know these women better than they know themselves. Luckily, these types of comments are far more typical *outside* of the workplace than within, so your time in the office should be relatively free of judgment on this count. (If it's not, refer to *Chapter 10*.)

OTHER WAYS OF GIVING BACK

Not everyone has children. I was at a dinner recently with three former colleagues of mine. Everyone was talking about what they've been up to, what their children are doing, grandchildren... The conversation moved to me and what I'm doing, and I talked about the various organizations I'm involved with and what we're doing. I was running through those things, and they all looked at each other and said, "What have we been doing? This is awful!" I said, "You know, you all had children, so you all had things that you needed to do. I had to go find something to help me give back".

Without children, I had more time to give. That's how I got involved with all of the various organizations that I did. A couple of things I've done are co-founding a charter school and being involved with a program for at-risk youth. I would say that I have had hundreds of children because I worked with hundreds of kids through those programs. – **Tina**

One more age-old assumption might crop up: If you're married, your husband is probably the primary breadwinner. This one is becoming less and less common, but, depending on your boss/HR personnel, you might even face lower pay because they assume that yours is just supplemental income. As the years go on, it might seem unlikely that you will ever face this bias, but keep your eyes open so that you recognize it if it ever happens to you.

Of course, not everyone is like this and not all of you will face any of these biases and double standards. A lot of progress has been made over the decades, and a lot of these ideas are dying out. If you do come into contact with archaic gender assumptions, though, remember that those do not create a good working environment. Different bosses will be more fair and equitable than others, so even changing departments within a company can make a huge difference in creating an equal playing field.

The progress that has been made and that we continue to make is good for everyone. As we push back on assumptions about childbearing, childrearing, and moneymaking, we free women to pursue their careers more successfully and more fairly, and we allow men to be better, more involved fathers and partners. Everyone deserves a fair work-life balance, and gender equality in the workplace promotes that.

IT *MUST* BE HORMONES

The work environment discourages showing your emotions. You are meant to always be polite and positive, and, especially in the case of women, behaving in any other manner is unacceptable. If you shed a single tear, peers and managers might think that you're too emotional and unable to handle the stresses of the job.

What about getting angry? Slamming doors and throwing things is never appropriate in the workplace, but, again, the penalty is greater for women than it is for men. When men do it, it's often considered normal. But if a woman does it, she's temperamental—or worse, hormonal.

> #### *BASELESS ACCUSATION*
> *One of my large projects was shipped overnight air, even though all of the order information directed ground freight. It was an unfortunate human error in our shipping department. You might imagine my surprise when the company owner called me into his office and was blaming me for the error.*
>
> *Even though I was agitated, I remained steady and asked how I could possibly have prevented the error. It was easy to sympathize with the owner, as the company would take a significant loss to the additional air freight cost. However, I would not accept the injustice of being*

> blamed for the error. During our discussion, I pointed out that I had never known him to egregiously blame a sales person for a clear production error. It was nonsense. By standing my ground and remaining calm, we moved forward. **– Lynn**

As always, when you see inequality in treatment, call it out. Point out that your expressions of emotion are normal behavior and that men in the office have done the same thing. Calmly and professionally bring the gender-based judgment to your manager's attention. They might not see it right away, but they will hopefully consider what you said and be more conscientious in the future.

MISCONSTRUED INTENTIONS

While women of reproductive age aren't allowed to get mad or sad at work, they're also not allowed to be friendly—at least, that's how it seems sometimes. The issues that exist in your general life also exist in the office.

First is the assumption that if you show genuine interest and kindness to a man, you must be trying to seduce him. There is a heteronormative assumption of sexual tension between men and women at work that feeds into the notion that a woman who smiles at a man and laughs at his jokes must be romantically/sexually interested in him. Obviously, this is not true. It's just women being polite, but intentions are frequently misconstrued in this situation.

We're all familiar with the story trope of a successful woman being assumed to have gotten her position by sleeping with the boss. Men are almost never accused of performing sexual favors in exchange for professional advancements, but women often are—especially if they're young and attractive. Not only is this double standard biased and untrue, it's also hurtful and risks the woman's reputation.

Friendliness and ambition are assumed indicators of seductive intent—and so are skirts. So what should you wear? Wear a pantsuit, and you're insufficiently feminine. Wear skirts that hit at the knee, and you're overtly sexual. A skirt that goes below the knee, of course, is prudish, and don't even think about going above the knee. With some workplaces that even require women to wear heels and make up, what are you to do?

Be yourself. Continue to be polite and friendly, but keep your distance with men (and women) who misconstrue your behavior to be seductive. Wear whatever meets your company's dress code and makes you feel comfortable. In the case of an unfair dress code, bring your concern to HR, and see if you can make flat shoes acceptable, for example.

Remember that colleagues who accuse you of sleeping with the boss or assume that you're trying to sleep with *them* are out of line. Bring it to your manager's attention if someone is making you feel uncomfortable. If it escalates to sexual harassment, follow the steps outlined in *Chapter 10*. These double standards are sexist and hurtful, and you don't have to stand for them.

FEMINIZING PROFESSIONALISM

Double standards need to be broken. The way to do this is *not* for women to be more like men in the office. It's to change the attitude within the workplace.

This isn't to say that we can't learn a few things from our male colleagues. Boys and girls tend to be raised differently, and the way boys are socialized can help them in the workplace when they become men. They are taught to ask for what they want, and so men will ask their bosses to consider them for promotions, and they are more likely to negotiate pay raises.

KNOW YOUR WORTH

This chapter would have been very helpful to me when I was young. When I was negotiating my compensation, I sold myself short. While I had checked with another individual I knew in a similar position at the company, I failed to make adjustments for my more favorable leverage position.

It took me several years of employment with the company to realize that the compensation for the various sales people was widely diverse. The individuals who were strong and assertive earned a lot more, even when their job performance did not match my own. While most of the top earners were men, there were two strong women who knew their worth and were compensated for it.

When I negotiated a raise, it wasn't much of a negotiation at all. I simply had to ask and state my reasons. The organization knew my value, but had no problem underpaying. When I asked for the raise, they could see I was serious and ready to walk.

What I learned laid the foundation of successfully negotiating my compensation for every job in my future. You need to know your value to the organization, and you need to be willing and ready to say no and walk away. This will give you a position of strength to negotiate. **– Lynn**

Remember that you are competent, professional, and powerful, and you deserve recognition. When you know that a position needs to be filled, ask to be considered for that promotion. If you feel that your work is deserving of higher compensation, say so and negotiate a new salary.

Still, the real key to breaking down double standards is to change the game. Business is often a boys' club, and leadership training is often targeted toward men. To counter this, women need to support each other and promote each other. Mentoring and organizations like the National Association of Professional Women (NAPW) and the American Business Women's Association (ABWA) are great ways for women to help each other up and make the office a little more equal.

Be brave, and point out double standards when you see them. Nothing will change until people know what's wrong. Managers will likely be defensive when you bring up their biases, but it's important that they consider their actions. If nothing changes, bring your manager's actions to the attention of HR.

The progress we've made since World War II has been tremendous, but it's taken us 70 years to get to this point. It will take more time to realize true equality in the workplace, but with each generation becoming bolder, millennials have the power to push business further in that direction than any generation before. Do your part to make that happen!

RECAP

Double standards are never acceptable, and they have no place in the office. This chapter discussed gender bias, but, for many women, the problems are compounded with racial, ethnic, religious, age, or sexual orientation or gender identity

bias. When facing bias in the workplace, ask yourself these questions:
1. Do you have to repeat yourself to be heard at work? Who should you address to make sure your ideas are acknowledged? How can you make your words more impactful?
2. Are you concerned about the assumptions interviewers might make about you if you're married? How does your boss react to you taking time off for your children compared to your male co-workers? How does your salary compare with your male co-workers'?
3. Are you able to express your emotions without fear of unfair judgment? Are temper tantrums tolerated when they come from male colleagues?
4. Is your kindness misconstrued as flirtations by your co-workers? Does the dress code seem fair at your office?
5. How can you promote yourself at work? Where can you find a support network of professional women?

PLAYLIST

Get ready to smash double standards by getting pumped up with a punchy playlist: http://p2q.link/chapter12

CHAPTER 13
LEADERSHIP STYLES

NEARLY EVERY WORKER has a boss. Whether you answer to the board of directors, the CEO, a mid-level manager, or a store manager, you probably have someone who you can consider your boss. Not all bosses are created equal, however. Different managers have different styles and motivations, and it's best for you to know which styles you work well with. Knowing your favorite leadership style will also help you be the best manager you can be when you are put in a leadership position.

LEADERSHIP STYLE CHECK

Throughout your career, you will face a lot of different leaderships styles among your bosses. Some will be wonderful, some will be terrible, and a lot will be just okay. A leader's job is to provide direction and motivation for the team, and some leaders are simply more effective at this in certain scenarios than others. Understanding the different leadership styles will help you decide how to respond to your various managers throughout your life. Each style has its pros and cons; it just depends on the situation and the needs of the employees.

There are six generally agreed upon forms of leadership: Directive, Authoritative, Affiliative, Participative, Pacesetting, and Coaching. The most effective of these styles depends on the field, company, and situation.

Directive leaders are what you think of when you envision military commanders. They tell you what to do, and they expect you to do it. The main source of motivation they provide is threat of punishment, and they tend to micromanage. This might sound unpleasant to some, but the style is the most efficient in times of crisis or when deviation can lead to serious risks. However, in times of stability, workers will likely become resentful of the treatment, and opportunities to develop new skills will be few and far between.

Next on the list are Authoritative managers; these are also called Visionary leaders. These leaders provide the direction (vision) for the team, and then allow the team to do the work. They will repeat the goal as frequently as necessary, but they typically allow the employees to go about reaching the goal in their own fashion. Authoritative leaders motivate their team through persuasion and praise. This all sounds great, but it's not always effective. This style does not provide much guidance to the team members or provide a lot of hands-on help. Furthermore, Visionary leaders must be credible—if the employees don't believe in the vision, they have no reason to work toward it.

Those focused on team harmony are Affiliative leaders. Above all else, they prioritize team building and connecting employees. While this is great at effecting a feeling of comradery among the team, it's not terribly efficient when it comes to getting tasks done, unless the work is rote. Affiliative managers are not ideal for crises or correcting problems.

Fourth are the Participative leaders. Also known as Democratic managers, they involve the entire team in the decision-making process. Every employee gets a vote on what gets done and when. This leadership style recognizes and utilizes the skills and expertise of the team. This is wonderful, but it can seriously slow down the progress of a project if every little decision requires a meeting and a vote. It can also be disastrous in times of crisis, or when employees lack the knowledge or training necessary to give educated votes.

Pacesetting managers tend to do a lot of the work themselves. This is because they are highly driven to achieve the best results in the least amount of time. They expect their team to follow their example and be self-motivated. If an employee doesn't perform well enough, their work is often taken away from them. This style works well for highly competent and driven teams, but is not ideal for employees that need more direct help or inspiration.

Finally, coaching leaders excel at developing their employees and their skills. They also try to connect the goals of the individual employees to the goals of the company. Team members are given the opportunity to learn new skills, as well as to teach other members the skills that they are good at. Coaches can tend to hold onto an underperforming employee rather than let them go, and their one-on-one development can be seen by some workers as micromanaging. Further, this leadership style is not effective in times of crisis or with unmotivated teams.

While these are the typical leadership types, you will also experience a few other types, combinations of styles, or extreme forms of the above categories. The first is one we covered in **Chapter 10**: bullies. They are demanding and harsh, and they can make your job a nightmare. You know you're working for a bully when they yell at you in person and over the phone, humiliate you in front of their peers, and blame you for their own mistakes. These are the worst kind of bosses and should be avoided when possible.

Related to bullies are authoritarian leaders. These bosses believe they know everything, and they have no interest in others' ideas. If you work for an authoritarian manager, you'll find that they want to control everything and are very strict with their rules.

On the other end of the spectrum are the bosses who are coddlers. Rules are not enforced, which is unfortunate, but at least these managers encourage feedback from their employees. You might find that people with this leadership style behave more like certain types of parents, trying to keep everyone happy at the cost of efficiency. You will rarely see this style in top leadership positions.

Sometimes you will have bosses that don't want to hear the bad news and bury their head in the sand when things start to go sideways. This guarantees that the problem won't get fixed, and the entire team will suffer. There are bosses that have an inferiority complex and only promote the mediocre workers so that they themselves will look better. Others will look for their employees to kiss up to them and reward only that kind of behavior.

The possibilities are endless. Many managers have multiple leadership style components; the best ones will modify their style as needed for any given situation. Generally, good bosses have high expectations, but also offer high support. Feedback is encouraged, but rules are enforced. Judgment is fair, and praise is forthcoming. This is the kind of boss that you will want to work for—they will challenge you to do your best work without running you ragged.

A DREAM COME TRUE
I had the good fortune of co-founding a charter school.

> *The Executive Director had a very specific vision about the culture she wanted within the school. That was that every child who walked into the school—this was K–5 at the time—would know that the expectation was that they were going to go to college. Every single day, they would be greeted, "Good morning, scholar." All of us on the board had our own strengths and leadership styles, but we all fell behind the Executive Director because of the strength of her leadership and her ability to communicate her vision.* **– Tina**

You might even work in an office that doesn't *have* set managers. No one is in charge, but everyone is in charge, in these environments. Leadership shifts according to the project and employees' strengths. This innovative method takes a bottom-up approach and allows the staff to present their own ideas and collaborate on projects. It might seem tricky, but this lack of leadership might work by inspiring you.

As you advance in your career, you will discover which types of leadership work well for you, which you can tolerate, and which you should avoid. Everyone's style is different, so look at the individual and decide what's best for you. And remember, working for someone with an opposing style will often foster your own growth by pushing you outside your comfort zone, so your process of self-discovery will be replete with opportunities to learn.

FIGHT OR FLIGHT

What should you do if you find yourself faced with a leadership style you can't stand? In the case of a bully, review *Chapter 10*. But what about everyone else? Do you keep your head down and muddle on through, or do you find your way to greener pastures?

Hopping from job to job every time you're faced with a manager you don't like is unrealistic and looks bad on your resume. Anyway, leaving for another corporation often isn't feasible... but you might be able to switch departments. However, the question remains: When should you flee a bad manager? We can't answer this question for you. It's a personal judgment that you will have to make, but consider the following: Does your boss make you feel anxious about your job? Is the leadership style causing your work to suffer significantly? Are you unable to move forward with your career under this leadership?

MISTRUSTFUL MANAGERS
For two years, I worked in a challenging environment. The managers were not mean, overly demanding, or bad people. It was challenging because the managers did not like sales people, pure and simple. It was strange since they had some really terrific sales people who were top performers with solid professionalism, and yet the organization had a constant churn of sales people—a problem that only affected that position within the company.

So, for two years, I tolerated the managers going through everything on my desk and through my files. I ignored the slights to the sales efforts objectives. I tamped down my frustration to get the job done. There were multiple meetings in which I worked to find middle ground. After the managers went to see my premier client without my knowledge and without my client's permission, I knew I could not continue to turn a blind eye to their odd behavior. Once I "woke up," I realized how much latent stress I had been bottling up because of the weirdness of my work situation and their management style. Moving on to a new organization was reinvigorating. **– Lynn**

You might have to answer to a manager whose leadership style isn't right for you. More often than not, your best move will be to adapt to the style. Take time to get used to your manager and try to understand how best to work with them. Ask your boss what their expectations are and how to be successful. Try to have that dialogue before you hightail it out of that department. Remember, adaptability is a good skill to have in any career, so see if you can make the best out of a less-than-ideal situation.

SUCCEEDING AS A LEADER
Sooner or later, you will have an opportunity to be a leader. As a manager or a project leader, it will become *your* job to provide direction and motivation to your team. Become

a leader *you* would want to work with. Be a leader who is effective and fair.

A good leader is clear about their expectations with firm but fair rules. As always, you should be reasonable with your team about goals and deadlines, and be responsive to their needs and problems your team may face. As a leader, your job is to push your team to do their best. Have high standards for your team and expect them to do their job competently and on time. If they don't understand something, it's reasonable to expect them to research the matter or ask questions. On the other hand, be supportive of them. Be encouraging and provide them with the resources they need to get the job done.

It's important to celebrate and appreciate employees who shine. Give credit where credit is due, and don't hold back praise for a job well done—positive reinforcement can work wonders! You will make that person's day by saying "thank you!" or "good work!" for a job well done. They will feel appreciated and take more ownership of the team's project and work harder. Everybody wins!

On your end, make sure that you are always honest with your team. Let them know the status of the project, what is going well, and what is not. Also, do what you say you will do, do it well, and do it in a timely manner. This way, you will demonstrate the behavior you expect from your team, and you will ward off feelings of resentment by avoiding double standards. It's important to show off your personal ethics by always being straightforward and professional. Leadership by example is the most powerful.

Part of this is not pretending that you know everything. You can't be the best at everything, so it's important to work with the best. Know enough to know when to bring in an expert—your team will appreciate your honesty and efficiency. If someone on your team has a particular strength, use it! If no one on your team has the knowledge that you need for a particular task, go outside of your team—even hire a specialist, if one is available to you. Hubris will get you nowhere, so ask for help when you need, just like you would expect your team to do.

GAINING CONFIDENCE IN OTHERS
Early in my career, I believed that everyone shared the same work ethic as I. It was a rude awakening to find

that others did not share my intention and specificity to approaching a project.

I found this to be frustrating and, of course, this compounded the situation. It was a huge lesson for me—to learn to respect differences in approach and differences in passion.

Once I realized my mistake, my team became more productive! Showing confidence in the ability of others to work at their own pace is something I always keep in mind. **– Tina**

When you find yourself being appointed to a leadership position, take Mufasa's advice and remember who you are. Be true to yourself and your style, and be kind and respectful to your team and everyone you work with. You don't need to erase your personality to be an effective leader. You just have to, as always, treat others how you would want to be treated.

As a true leader, you must see the big picture, analyze and assess situations from all angles, and utilize insights to predict outcomes. You achieve this by listening to new and alternative ideas. While you leverage your hard-earned experience and knowledge, recognize that change is constant. What worked yesterday will not necessarily continue to be the best solution. Creating a vibrant environment for your team to challenge paradigms will keep you all moving forward.

Leaders usually get most of the credit or the blame for a project. You need to look out for yourself and make sure that things go well, but keep a balance—don't take advantage of others to save your own skin. Do what's best for you, your family, and your career, but always stay true to your ethics.

RUDE VS. ASSERTIVE

To be an effective leader, you need to be assertive—but never rude. The line between assertive and rude can be a fine one, especially with women. Women are in the unique position of needing to be perceived as neither "weak" nor "bitchy," which can be tough to do. You can't change people's gender biases, but you can present your best self.

RUDE AWAKENING

While I was managing a team, it became obvious

that I was not working well with one team member. I reached out to my boss for advice and insight on how to resolve the issue. We talked through my concerns, and my boss asked my permission to speak with my team member.

My boss conveyed the key concerns from the team member: My style was too abrupt and demanding, and I did not explain why I wanted things done. I was not surprised; my challenges with the team member were on performance, or, more accurately, the lack thereof. While I tried to be clear on expectations, I recognized that my frustrations with the employee were making me borderline rude and ineffective.

My boss helped me see that when you briefly explain why you want something done, it no longer seems arbitrary. The experience I gained made a real difference for my leadership style moving forward. I learned to explain my reasons for wanting something done a certain way, to listen and consider alternatives, and to address performance challenges immediately and proactively. **– Lynn**

While you should never take advantage of your team, never let an employee—or anyone else—take advantage of you. Remember that assertiveness comes from a place of strength, not insecurity. You want to make known your feelings, values, or stance because you know you deserve to be heard. It also leaves room for conversation, while rudeness aims to shut down the conversation. Show that you are ready to step up to a challenge.

THAT'S WHAT IT'S ALL ABOUT
This isn't a work story, but it deals with leadership. When I was in high school, I was captain of the color guard, which performs with the marching band. During a Saturday morning practice with the entire band, my teammates were obviously testy—they snapped at each other and argued over who is meant to be where. The entire team was frustrated, and asking them to be polite to each other was no help.

Suddenly, I had an idea. I signaled the color guard to go to the far side of the football field, away from the rest of the band. I instructed them to form of a circle, and then informed them that we would be doing the Hokey Pokey. They were confused, but they trusted me, so we all began putting our hands, feet, and heads in and out and shaking it all about. Soon, the whole team was laughing and smiling. After only a few minutes away from the practice, I brought them back to the band, and the rest of practice went off without a hitch. Sometimes you just need to relieve some stress to get back to being kind. **– Rachel**

Rudeness might come out when you're tired, hungry, or stressed. Humans are emotional creatures, and it's natural for us to have bad days. Just remember that we are all people and consider how your words and actions might affect your team. If a team member does something wrong, comment on the action without commenting on them as a person. Stay civil, stay positive, but don't back down.

RECAP
Throughout your career, you will find yourself as a team member and leader at varying times. In both cases, knowing which kind of leadership style you work well with is important to being an effective employee. When figuring out what you look for in a leader and what kind of leader you want to be, ask yourself the following questions:

1. Does your boss value input from their team members? Are your manager's expectations challenging but fair? How does your boss handle criticism?
2. Are you unable to work effectively under your manager? Is another position available for you, within or outside of the company? How can you adapt to your manager's style?
3. Do you challenge your team to do the best work possible? How do you show your appreciation for a job well done? What methods do you use to be an effective leader?
4. How can you identify when you're being assertive vs. when you're being rude? How can you keep others' feelings in perspective?

PLAYLIST
Remember, you were born to lead. The right music will get you in a commanding mindset: http://p2q.link/chapter13

CHAPTER 14
FIND FULFILLMENT & FEED YOUR SOUL

MANY PEOPLE SHARE a common goal: finding fulfillment at work. The old adage tells us that "if you do what you love, you'll never work a day in your life." That sounds lovely and is certainly a feeling to aspire to, but the fact is that most of us *do* work. Most of us don't love our jobs—some of us don't even *like* our jobs—but we spend a lot of our time there. What can you do to make your work more gratifying?

MAKING WORK FUN
First of all, remember that there is almost always something fulfilling about your job. Not all of us can work to save the world each day, but almost everyone can find something in their job that makes them feel good about themselves in one way or another.

It's easy to get bogged down and bored with what you're doing, especially if your job is rote. Just keep in mind that there are a lot of ways that you can get engaged, excited, and passionate about what you're doing. Appreciate the team you work with, the work that you do, the environment that you work in, or any other positive aspect of your job. Maybe all you do is data entry, but keep in mind all the important things that higher-ups are doing with your hard work.

DRIVING AWAY THE STRESS
During tradeshow season, everything would get very tense and stressful in the marketing department—so many tasks, deadlines, and interdependencies to stay in front of! We all needed a break, but it seemed impossible with so much to get done.

One sunny afternoon, I insisted we all go outside for a breath of fresh air. In the parking lot, I had a set up race lanes with duct tape. Everyone opened up the brightly colored toy cars I had given them. We proceeded to race the cars. Within a few short minutes, everyone was smiling, laughing, and shaking off the stress. After 20 minutes, we went back to our desks with our race cars and a fresh perspective. Those cars remained on everyone's desk, and over the next two weeks, we would take breaks to race the cars in the parking lot.

All of our tradeshows turned out great that season.
– Lynn

Find a way to add your personal flair to your work. Communicate in a creative, thought-provoking way. Decorate your desk. There will always be mundane things that you need to do for your job, so try to find a way to make them fun—listen to music or set small goals for yourself. Finding fulfillment can be as simple as making a to-do list and checking items off—there is a strong sense of satisfaction that can give.

Meet people at your company. Say hello to everyone, and see if you can find someone you connect with. It's easier to enjoy your job if you like and respect the people that you work with. Being proud of your company is a great way to feel more fulfilled at your job, and a good path to get there is being proud of its employees.

Look for opportunities to expand your skillset. Volunteer to take on new projects or to develop competencies that your team needs. Not only will this give you stimulation at your job, it will make you more competitive if you decide to seek out a new position.

Finally, remember to actually *leave* work every day; take your mind off of your job once your shift is over. Only take on as much as you can handle. Resist working all night because of someone else's emergency. If you do this, know that there will always be another emergency, and people will get used to you being the one to fix it. Set your boundaries so that you don't become resentful of your colleagues.

If you become bitter, fulfillment will be much harder to achieve. So stand up for yourself, and set your boundaries. Manage your own work, take care of yourself, and respect yourself and your time. Be professional and assertive about your parameters, and you will be valued and respected by your managers and peers.

GETTING INVOLVED

Beyond the day-to-day grind, see if there are other ways to get involved at your job. There might be activities that you can take part in—maybe you can organize a craft fair or company picnic. Maybe you can be on the committee for Fun Fridays. If your company has such programs, there are little things that you can get involved with that will make you more engaged with your peers and company.

> ### BUDDING RELATIONSHIPS
> *A woman I worked with gave tulip bulbs to her clients every fall. It was a great idea, so the next year I suggested all the sales people participate as a company promotion. We got all the supplies together and booked the conference room. All the sales people got together to pack their bulb promos. While we talked a lot about work, we also just talked. I got to know people better in those few hours than the during the several years I had worked with them before.* **– Lynn**

Of course, you don't need to take the lead to take part. Help with one-day events, like packing backpacks for children in need. You don't have to be a program chair to participate and feel good. Still, you should make sure that you actually contribute. Instead of being just a warm body, demonstrate your skills and leadership by doing well and helping others.

Outside of your company, you can join organizations in your field. Attend conferences with people with similar jobs to get insight into how you can do your work better and feel more fulfilled. These are people who are happy to help and whom you can help in return, which will also make you feel engaged. The opportunities are endless to connect with people inside and outside your company.

LOOKING UP

Everyone has to start somewhere, and many of us will begin on the lowest rung of the corporate ladder—or whichever ladder you're on. It might feel like you're far away from all the creative, fulfilling work, but remember that you can make it to that level.

Go upstairs, and introduce yourself to the people who do what you want to be doing. If you're a receptionist, you're at an advantage because you likely see and greet these people every day. *Chapter 7* discussed networking in detail, but what we didn't stress is networking within your own company. Making connections with people in the department you aspire to can help you get that dream job. Many companies prefer to hire and promote from within, so those links can help you a lot over the years. Let the people in that department know what you'd like to be doing, and ask if there is any way that you can help. Your assistance might start small, but they will come to trust you and your judgment.

Say yes to every opportunity you can. Show your manager and the people in the department you want to move to that you are eager take part in projects and that you produce good work. Show off your skills every chance you get, and learn new skills by taking on these new responsibilities. Your expanding portfolio and resume will help you climb the ranks within your company or at another company.

Keep in mind that starting from the bottom can help you in the long term. While the work might seem mundane now, as you work your way up, you will have an understanding of the company and all its moving parts unparalleled by those who started higher up. Your peers will seek out your wisdom, and you will be an integral part of the team once you reach the department you want to be in. So, don't despair! You are learning skills and knowledge that you will need to be successful once your reach your dream job.

WHEN A JOB IS JUST A JOB

Sometimes, of course, your fulfillment simply won't come from your job. You may have ended up in this position due to a financial decision—you needed to pay the bills, and this was the job available. Most of us have been there. Or maybe you have no intention of ever using your career as a source of satisfaction, and you plan to get fulfillment elsewhere.

The first thing to do is to recognize that you've made the conscious decision to take this job, and give yourself permission to be okay with that choice. You had your reasons, and you did what was best for you. Respect yourself for that. A job is not a marker of you or your worth, so don't let yourself or anyone else make your feel embarrassed for it, either.

While in this position, temporary or not, you will have to make the most of it. You will usually be able to find at least one colleague that you can connect with. That person makes the shift bearable, so cultivate that relationship, and be each other's cheerleaders. Make a list of pros and cons about your job, and try to concentrate on those positives. There are times the positive can be as small as "pays the rent" and "sometimes someone brings donuts".

If you do plan to eventually find gratification through work, think of your current job as a stepping stone to where you will be. In the meantime, learn new skills and network. If you don't know exactly what you want to do, try to find out! If you can, test out different tasks at your current job, or volunteer somewhere that will allow you to try something new, or just read about it at your local library and online. There are options for you, and you will find that fulfilling job if you keep looking.

On the other hand, if your job is simply a way to keep you financially afloat while you follow your passions and find fulfillment elsewhere, own it. Many of us want our careers to be a source of gratification, but not everyone does. If you want to be good at your job, have a pleasant experience while you're there, but leave it all behind at the end of your shift and get your satisfaction from other parts of life, that's okay! Don't let anyone tell you what you should consider important.

Keep in mind that work alone can't fulfill you. Who are you? What else do you do? Do you make music, volunteer, or read? Find fulfillment through your hobbies, activism, and/or friends. There are a lot of facets to every person, so make sure you are expressing all of them and living your best life. Don't let a disappointing job keep you from living a happy, fulfilled life.

REDISCOVERING YOUR PASSIONS
When I was in college, I was involved with politics and the international community. I participated in the Model United Nations, which I absolutely loved. But when I got out of college and started working, one thing led to another, and I lost sight of those things that really compelled me. It didn't dawn on me that I could try to incorporate that into my life.

I had a working colleague that invited me to a series called "Town Hall: Los Angeles" that featured both business and political leaders that would present, typically during a luncheon. It reconnected me with that side of my personality and interests that I hadn't thought about in so long. It was through this speaker series that I was introduced to like-minded people.

Through that experience I became involved in the non-profit arena. I made time to do all those things that were of interest to me in college—and high school, for that matter—but had gotten lost along the way. I encourage anyone who has an opportunity to go back and explore an area that they may have forgotten about. **– Tina**

RECAP

Most of us want to find gratification through our work. Even if you don't have your dream job, you can probably find some fulfillment in what you do. When trying to find ways to feel satisfied at work, ask yourself the following questions:

1. What do you appreciate about your job? How can you add your personal flair to your work? What are the boundaries that you should set?
2. Does your company have charity or fun organizations? How can you get involved? What organizations can you join in your field?
3. Who do you want to work with? How can you help the department you want to work in?
4. Why did you choose this job? Who can you connect with at work? What do you do outside of work to find gratification?

PLAYLIST

Set the tone for your success story by listening to the lush soundscapes of our playlist: http://p2q.link/chapter14

CONCLUSION

You've reached the end of *Practical Wisdoms @ Work*—congratulations! We hope your journey through this book has provided insights and ideas that will help you build your career and reach your goals. Revisit these pages any time you face a new challenge, and ask yourself the questions in our chapter recaps. This volume will be a resource to you for years to come.

MAIN LESSONS FROM THE BOOK
Throughout this book, we have related our hard-earned experience through advice and stories. We endeavored to be specific to the challenge, whether it's with time management or workplace bullies. After all, it's usually best to tailor the advice to the situation! Still, there are a few principles that you can carry with you throughout your career.

KNOW YOURSELF AND BE TRUE TO YOURSELF
In order to choose your path, you need to know yourself—your strengths, values, and goals. What you are good at or have a natural talent for can inform you of which careers you are most likely to succeed in. Your values can guide the type of causes and people you want to work for and which practices you prefer. And your goals—those are your dreams, where you want to be in the future. Once you are certain of these things, the way forward will become clearer.

For some people, this self-awareness comes easily, but others have to work hard for self-discovery. Even if you think you know yourself, it helps to ask yourself questions. Finding out how you best communicate, which environments enable you to be most efficient, and which leadership styles you work best under will help you find your place in the workforce.

A lot of this is learned through trial and error, and that's okay! Life is a journey of learning, and you discover more and more about yourself along the way, even as parts of you keep growing and shifting. So be sure to check in with yourself periodically; ask how you're doing, what you like and dislike, and where you want to be in a year—or five or ten.

The second part of this principle is that, once you know yourself, you need to be true to yourself. Being flexible within your career is a great way to be a team player and take advantage of new opportunities. Compromising your core values, however, or veering too far away from a path that leads to your goals can leave you feeling unfulfilled and burned out. Remember who you are and what you stand for throughout your career, but be sure to leave yourself room to grow.

BE KIND

Be respectful to everyone you encounter in business. A person's title or employment status have no bearing on their entitlement to respect. Honor the work and service of each colleague, client, and employee by being warm, patient, and understanding. After all, no one can be their best all of the time!

Your goal should be to leave people feeling good, in addition to gathering or transmitting whatever information you need to. Besides the simple pleasure of making someone's day brighter, you can find satisfaction in the knowledge that people who feel appreciated work harder and are more helpful. It's a win for everybody to always be kind.

People will remember how you make them feel. If you make them feel good, they will be more eager to connect and collaborate with you, which is necessary to building a strong network. Remember that a professional network is your group of contacts that help each other and want each other to succeed. Being kind is necessary to building a supportive community, which open up opportunities.

ASK FOR HELP AND PAY IT FORWARD

If there is one message to take away from this book, it's that you don't have to go it alone. No matter what challenge you're facing, there is someone who has faced the same or a similar problem before you. Look around you, and see who might have some insight.

Overall, people are happy to help. As long as you're not interrupting when you ask for advice, your peers will likely be generous with their aid. Of course, it helps to ask politely, and to be specific about the challenge. With practice, you will become good at asking for help, and you will find that it's typically more efficient to ask someone for help rather than struggle with a task or situation on your own.

As you advance in your career and face (and receive advice on) a myriad of challenges, you will accrue a collection of practical wisdoms yourself. When this happens, don't hoard your knowledge—share it! Recall that you faced obstacles when you were starting out in your career, and offer your advice to newcomers and peers.

Becoming a mentor might be fulfilling for you. Check to see if your company offers a mentorship program, or look at outside professional mentorship organizations. Being a mentor allows you to watch a younger/less experienced professional grow into the potential you know they have. Playing a guiding role in their development might provide you with great satisfaction.

Regardless of whether you become a formal mentor or simply share your wisdom on a casual basis, sharing your bounty of experience will pay forward the help you received and continue to receive from those who have guided you. Here at Petite2Queen, we believe in women helping each other up the ladder.

THANK YOU

We hope you have found our initial volume of *Practical Wisdoms @ Work* valuable. When writing this book, our goal was to provide ideas for inspiration, out-of-the-box thinking, and a new way to shake your paradigms. By sharing our hard-earned knowledge, we hope that you can avoid our mistakes and accelerate your career success. Thank you for supporting us as we give voice to our opinions, and promoting our enduring vision to obliterate (or at least soften) barriers for women at work.

We're looking forward to continuing to help you along your journey. Follow us and join the conversation at Petite2Queen.com. **– Lynn and Tina**

ABOUT THE AUTHORS

KRISTINA M. OLSON
Kristina M. Olson is the co-founder and co-CEO of Petite2Queen. She is a business development leader with proven success and established expertise in sales strategies, strategic planning, integrated marketing strategies, and brand communications with global execution across multiple channels. Having held senior executive positions in a number of respected companies, she has developed strong client and network relationships with a hands-on approach to create solutions for short- and long-term strategic opportunities.

Success in the business world has afforded Kristina the ability to share those skills towards her social passions of education, at-risk youth, and homelessness. At Petite2Queen, Kristina is focused on sharing her knowledge and experience to assist women in their personal journey of growth and enlightenment.

LYNN M. WHITBECK
Lynn M. Whitbeck is the co-founder and co-CEO of Petite2Queen. Building on her 30 years of successes and experiences as Vice President of Business Development and COO of direct consumer technology start-ups, Lynn transitioned to executive consulting providing strategic expertise for the development and management of client programs. With this real-world background, Lynn brings a marketing, sales, business development, and operations management cross-sector experience to Petite2Queen.

At Petite2Queen, she is focused on identifying and evaluating opportunities for women at work, helping them define their personal roadmap in the long-, mid-, and short-term. She dedicates herself to delivering tangible and sustainable tools and insights to women, embracing visualization of the big picture, and identifying and implementing the minutiae of detail. Lynn's goal is to share the lessons learned along her journey and enable positive change for women.

RACHEL H. WHITBECK

Rachel H. Whitbeck is the Director of Operations and Communications at Petite2Queen. She earned her master's degree in Race, Ethnicity, and Conflict in 2016 from Trinity College Dublin, where she focused her research on the crossroads of gender, sexual orientation, and race. Rachel uses her experience in writing and editing books and articles, as well as her skills in research, to create content that appeals to and is reflective of the diverse millennial cohort.

REFERENCES

INTRODUCTION
[1] "10 Findings about Women in the Workplace," *Pew Research Center*, December 11, 2013. http://www.pewsocialtrends.org/2013/12/11/10-findings-about-women-in-the-workplace/. Last accessed April 7, 2017.

[2, 5, & 6] "On Pay Gap, Millennial Women Near Parity – For Now," *Pew Research Center*, December 11, 2013. http://www.pewsocialtrends.org/2013/12/11/on-pay-gap-millennial-women-near-parity-for-now/. Last accessed April 7, 2017.

[3] Richard Fry, "Millennials overtake Baby Boomers as America's largest generation," *Pew Research Center*, April 25, 2016. http://www.pewresearch.org/fact-tank/2016/04/25/millennials-overtake-baby-boomers/. Last accessed April 7, 2017.

[4] "The Young Professional Workforce," Department for Professional Employees, 2017. http://dpeaflcio.org/programs-publications/issue-fact-sheets/the-young-professional-workforce/. Last accessed April 7, 2017.

CHAPTER 1: EMBARKING ON YOUR JOURNEY
[1] Derek Thompson, "Work is Work: Why Free Internships Are Immoral," *The Atlantic*, May 14, 2012. https://www.theatlantic.com/business/archive/2012/05/work-is-work-why-free-internships-are-immoral/257130/. Last accessed April 7, 2017.

[2] Lauren Weber and Melissa Korn, "Where Did All the Entry-Level Jobs Go?" *The Wall Street Journal*, August 6, 2014. http://www.wsj.com/articles/want-an-entry-level-job-youll-need-lots-of-experience-1407267498. Last accessed April 7, 2017.

[3] Travis Mitchell. "Chart: See 20 Years of Tuition Growth at National Universities," *U.S. News*, July 29, 2015. http://www.usnews.com/education/best-colleges/paying-for-college/articles/2015/07/29/chart-see-20-years-of-tuition-growth-at-national-universities. Last accessed April 7, 2017.

[4] Kyle McCarthy, "10 Fun Facts About the Student Debt Crisis," *The Huffington Post*, January 22, 2014. http://www.huffingtonpost.com/kyle-mccarthy/10-fun-facts-about-student-loan-debt_b_4639044.html. Last accessed April 7, 2017.

[5] Drew DeSilver, "For most workers, real wages have barely budged for decades," *Pew Research Center*, October 9, 2014. http://www.pewresearch.org/fact-tank/2014/10/09/for-most-workers-real-wages-have-barely-budged-for-decades/. Last accessed April 7, 2017.

CHAPTER 4: WORK-LIFE BALANCE & BOUNDARIES

[1] "The 2015 Workplace Flexibility Study," *Workplace Trends*, February 3, 2015. http://workplacetrends.com/the-2015-workplace-flexibility-study/. Last accessed April 7, 2017.

[2] Nichole Bernier, "How Planners Maximize the Benefits of Telecommuting," *PCMA Convene*, August 1, 2016. http://www.pcmaconvene.org/features/cmp-series/how-meeting-planners-are-maximizing-the-benefits-of-telecommuting/. Last accessed April 7, 2017.

[3] "Latest Telecommuting Statistics," *Global Workplace Analytics*, January 2016. http://globalworkplaceanalytics.com/telecommuting-statistics. Last accessed April 7, 2017.

[4] "American Time Use Survey Summary," Bureau of Labor Statistics, June 24, 2016. http://www.bls.gov/news.release/atus.nr0.htm. Last accessed April 7, 2017.

[5 & 6] Kim Parker and Wendy Wang, "Modern Parenthood," *Pew Research Center*, March 14, 2013. http://www.pewsocialtrends.org/2013/03/14/modern-parenthood-roles-of-moms-and-dads-converge-as-they-balance-work-and-family/. Last accessed April 7, 2017.

[7] Carol Hymowitz, "Behind Every Great Woman," *Bloomberg*, January 5, 2012. http://www.bloomberg.com/news/articles/2012-01-04/behind-every-great-woman. Last accessed April 7, 2017.

CHAPTER 7: NETWORKING

[1] Frigyes Karinthy, "Chains," *Everything is Different* (1929).

CHAPTER 10: BULLYING & HARASSMENT AT WORK

[1] "Harassment," U.S. Equal Employment Opportunity Commission.

https://www.eeoc.gov/laws/types/harassment.cfm. Last accessed April 7, 2017.

[2] Alanna Vagianos, "1 In 3 Women Has Been Sexually Harassed At Work, According to Survey," *The Huffington Post*, February 19, 2015. http://www.huffingtonpost.com/2015/02/19/1-in-3-women-sexually-harassed-work-cosmopolitan_n_6713814.html. Last accessed April 7, 2017.

CHAPTER 12: BREAKING DOUBLE STANDARDS

[1] Dr. Stacey L. Smith and Crystal Allene Cook, "Gender Stereotypes: An Analysis of Popular Films and TV," The Geena Davis Institute on Gender in Media, 2008. http://seejane.org/wp-content/uploads/GDIGM_Gender_Stereotypes.pdf. Last accessed April 7, 2017.

[2] Melissa Hattab, Chancellor Gaffney, and Tabitha Belkorchi, interview with Jacki Lynden, "Casting Call: Hollywood Needs More Women," All Things Considered, *NPR*, June 30, 2013. http://www.npr.org/templates/transcript/transcript.php?storyId=197390707. Last accessed April 7, 2017.

[3] "Language Myth #6," PBS, 2005. http://www.pbs.org/speak/speech/prejudice/women/. Last accessed April 7, 2017.

[4] Leslie Shore, "Gal Interrupted, Why Men Interrupt Women And How To Avert This In The Workplace," January 3, 2017. http://www.forbes.com/sites/womensmedia/2017/01/03/gal-interrupted-why-men-interrupt-women-and-how-to-avert-this-in-the-workplace/#67b0e1ee5fba. Last accessed April 7, 2017.

www.ingramcontent.com/pod-product-compliance
Lightning Source LLC
Chambersburg PA
CBHW050538300426
44113CB00012B/2166